THE
"BABY DOLLS"

THE
"BABY DOLLS"

BREAKING *the* **RACE** *and* **GENDER BARRIERS**
of the **NEW ORLEANS MARDI GRAS TRADITION**

KIM MARIE VAZ

LOUISIANA STATE UNIVERSITY PRESS)|(BATON ROUGE

Published by Louisiana State University Press
Copyright © 2013 by Louisiana State University Press
All rights reserved
Manufactured in the United States of America
LSU Press Paperback Original
First printing

DESIGNER: Mandy McDonald Scallan
TYPEFACE: Calluna
PRINTER: McNaughton & Gunn, Inc.
BINDER: Dekker Bookbinding

Library of Congress Cataloging-in-Publication Data

Vaz, Kim Marie.
  The "Baby Dolls" : breaking the race and gender barriers of the New Orleans Mardi Gras tradition / Kim Marie Vaz.
    p. cm.
  Includes bibliographical references and index.
  ISBN 978-0-8071-5070-2 (pbk. : alk. paper) — ISBN 978-0-8071-5071-9 (pdf) — ISBN 978-0-8071-5072-6 (epub) — ISBN 978-0-8071-5073-3 (mobi)
  1. Carnival—Louisiana—New Orleans—History. 2. African American women—Louisiana—New Orleans—History. 3. African American women—Louisiana—New Orleans—Social conditions. 4. New Orleans (La.)—Social life and customs. 5. New Orleans (La.) —Race relations. I. Title.
  GT4211.N4V39 2013
  394.250976335—dc23

                                                          2012023994

In memory of my great-grandmother, Virginia Bender Glover

Who is this Baby Doll, and why is she
referred to as such? This is her story.
—*Robert McKinney, February 9, 1940*

contents

ILLUSTraTIONS

PreLuDe
On Being an Example of Hope

MARDI GRAS maskers of the Baby Doll tradition began as a small group of determined, independent-minded Black Creole women of New Orleans who came together and rebelled against the many constraints they faced regarding social segregation and gender discrimination. With an immeasurable love of freedom, on every Mardi Gras Day, groups of Black women and some men became the Baby Dolls and would parade, sing, and dance while representing their independent free spirit.

This Baby Doll tradition of women maskers was conceived and created around 1912. There are multiple stories of origin that are presented in my video documentary work, in this book by Kim Vaz, and in our collective work educating tourists, schoolchildren, locals, and scholars. We aim to tell the story of the key role the early Baby Dolls played in shaping New Orleans's cultural traditions. The origins of Black Storyville are better known, but the unknown story is told by the family of the late Alma "Karro" Trepagnier-Batiste. Ms. Karro was a Mardi Gras reveler and matriarch of one of New Orleans's most popular musical families: the Batiste family (original Sixth Ward), with its Dirty Dozen Kazoo Band. In the old New Orleans Mardi Gras traditions of the Black Creole societies, the Baby Dolls were celebrated right along with the Mardi Gras Indians, the Skeletons, and the parade krewe of Zulu. We have found that, from the beginning, the Baby Dolls were also referred to as the "women of the jazz." As jazz entrepreneurs, these women were a fixture in the downtown streets of old New Orleans not only on Mardi Gras but every day.

Today, wherever the Baby Dolls appear, whether on Mardi Gras, on

Super Sunday, or at the Satchmo second-line parade salute, locals tell us about their grandmothers who were Baby Dolls. Little children get excited and tug at the sleeve of the elder and ask, "Who is that Baby Doll?" And they always ask, "Can I dance with them?" The familiar reply is, "Those are Baby Dolls, but those are women."

Resurrecting this cultural practice has been good for the local community and the women who continue the tradition. It lifts up our hearts as we inspire others by dancing the route of the Zulu parade or participating in the second lines, in venues where we educate children, the community, and tourists about the tradition. We are following in the footsteps of the original Baby Dolls. Our giving back to the community by teaching our song and dance traditions follows the lead of the earlier generation, such as Alma Batiste, Miriam Batiste Reed, "Uncle" Lionel Batiste, Merline Kimble, and Resa "Cinnamon Black" Wilson-Bazile, a self-proclaimed "renegade" Baby Doll. We pay our respects to the late Antoinette K-Doe and her Ernie K-Doe Baby Dolls and the throngs of neighborhood Baby Dolls who masked in by-gone eras—such as the Big Queen of the Wild Tchoupitoulas, Mercedes Stevenson, who masked as a Baby Doll with two of her friends in the 1970s.

Through our professional dance organization, the New Orleans Society of Dance's Baby Doll Ladies have resurrected this unique tradition of live art and celebration of life, incorporating a teaching mission. In connecting with our elders, we bring to them and others happiness and affirmation. This tradition was shown to us by Ms. Batiste-Reed and "Uncle" Lionel Batiste, daughter and son of the late Alma "Karro" Trepagnier-Batiste, and by Geannie Thomas and Eva Perry of the K-Doe Baby Dolls. In this book, you will meet other Baby Dolls who have paraded in the streets through thick and thin: Resa "Cinnamon Black" Wilson-Bazile, Merline Kimble, and Lois Nelson.

When Uncle Lionel Batiste made bonnets for me by hand, and his sister, Ms. Miriam, shared the history and customs of the Baby Dolls with our group, we became the new generation of Baby Dolls. We are carrying the torch of our ancestral traditions. The costuming, dancing, parading, and pageantry are crafts and art forms handed down through the generations— a responsibility that these Baby Doll Ladies don't take lightly. Much like our forebears, contemporary Baby Doll groups personify womanhood through dance. The diversity in the creative and vernacular expressions of the current Baby Doll tradition by the city's various groups is dedicated to representing the uninhibited spirit of New Orleans with the same determination, perseverance, and attitude of excellence in all endeavors that was true for our predecessors. The reader will witness the Baby Doll tradition from the perspective of the old as well as the new. All generations of Baby Dolls demonstrate the smart and sassy attitude of excellence that is synonymous with New Orleans's women of the jazz, then and now.

Millisia White
Founder and Director, New Orleans Society of Dance, Inc.

Foreword

Black Storyville

As we got off the car, I looked straight down Liberty Street. Crowds of people were moving up and down as far as my eyes could see.
—Louis Armstrong on his arrival in Black Storyville as a young boy

BLACK STORYVILLE was the poor person's version of the famed Storyville red-light district a short distance away, perhaps without the fine champagne. It was within walking distance to the French Quarter, the Central Business District, and Central City. The ordinance establishing Black Storyville identified specific streets on which otherwise illegal activities such as gambling and prostitution could take place. These were Tulane, Gravier, Perdido, North Poydras, South Poydras, and Lafayette paralleling Canal Street, and streets going from the river toward the lake, roughly Saratoga, South Franklin, South Liberty, Howard, and Freret stretched forth in parallel.

While characterized largely as a site of moral degeneracy, the area housed a number of institutions that offered educational, social, and religious sustenance for its residents. Louis Armstrong, the neighborhood's most famous son, lived directly across the street from Fisk School for Boys at 507 South Franklin. Later in his life, Armstrong wrote appreciatively of the school, where he learned to read, write, and absorb musical styles and rhythms as the school staged operettas, developed choirs, and supported Creole musicians as teachers. He recalled childhood pastimes that included playing street games such as coon-can and craps, and having brick wars with his friends. He grew up around characters nicknamed Cocaine Buddy, Little Head Lucas, Egg Head Papa, Sister Pop, One-eyed Bud, Black Benny, Nicodemus, Dirty Dog, and Steel-Armed Johnny.

Four buildings down from Armstrong's house was the United Sons of Honor Hall, the home of a benevolent association incorporated on February 12, 1868, to assist the sick, bury the dead, and "attend to the distressed widows and succor the orphans of its members." As much as the area was known for its pleasure industries, it supported not only the profane but also the sacred. Churches abounded to satisfy the spiritual hunger of the residents. Mount Zion Baptist Church stood at 512 Howard Street, led by the Reverend George Poole. Wesley Chapel Methodist-Episcopal Church (Negro), the Wesleyan Chapel Hall, and a rectory located in the 400 block of South Liberty were places of note. In Black Storyville, many women worked as laundresses, some as seamstresses and hairdressers. Some women ran boardinghouses and restaurants either alone or with their husbands. Those men who did not own businesses were laborers working on steamboats and in coal yards, sugar plants, sawmills, and blacksmith shops.

Local residents worked hard and played hard. South Rampart Street was the high-energy entertainment strip. Vic Dubois's Union Station Exchange Restaurant and Bar was at 836 South Rampart; Mrs. F. J. Luins ran the Union Lodging House at 719 South Rampart; Porters Exchange Restaurant was nearby at 1000 Perdido, as was the Liberty Liquor House at 1332 Perdido. The Original Panama House at 328 South Liberty offered rooms with or without board. On South Saratoga Street (now 234 Loyola), the still-standing Pythian Temple housed Black professional offices and hosted theatrical productions, musical offerings, and other events in the building's "Theatorium." The Pythian Temple, a towering and impressive piece of architecture, was the location of ground-breaking cultural innovations. Early New Orleans jazz legends such as Sidney Bechet, Papa Celestin's Original Jazz Orchestra, and Kid Rena performed there. In addition to music, there was theatrical invention. About 1909, a play by a group called the Smart Set titled *There Is and Never Will Be a King like Me,* about a Zulu king, was staged at the Pythian. The performance and its content so captured the imagination of a group of Black male friends who masked on Carnival that they transformed their image of themselves from "tramps" to "kings" (literally as portraying African royalty). They called their reinvented group "the Zulus."

The neighborhood was rough-and-tumble, especially after the passage of the city ordinance officially designating certain blocks of this Black neighborhood as a legalized vice district. As such, it attracted the unsavory. Yet, as Armstrong wrote, "Bad men liked good music."

The neighborhood, with its prominent intersection of South Liberty and Perdido streets, played a prominent place in the lives of the residents. These "hot thoroughfares" came to be embodied in music with recordings such as "Liberty & Perdido," "Perdido Street Blues," and "New Orleans Stomp." The neighborhood's brick and cobblestone streets reverberated with the feet of marching clubs and brass bands that broadcast the streets' rambunctious sounds. There was the Tammany's Social and Pleasure Club, the Bulls, Hobgoblins, and the Zulu Club. Others who paraded through Black Storyville included the Young Men Twenties, Merry Go Rounds, Tulane Club, Young Men Vidalias, Money Wasters, the Jolly Boys, and the Million Dollar Baby Dolls.

The Million Dollar Baby Dolls came into being in the same neighborhood that nurtured Louis Armstrong. Though women's groups abounded, none offered anything as unusual as the Carnival theatrics of the Million Dollar Baby Dolls. Like many representing the extant New Orleans street-culture legacy that arose from Black Storyville, this group of women managed to maintain their earliest traditions, re-create them Carnival season after Carnival season, and delight and seduce Mardi Gras goers every year. Back then, the women were rowdy, bawdy, and competitive. Today, they are professional dancers, seamstresses, choreographers, teachers, and nurses who resurrected the tradition and re-create a 1912 Black Storyville Mardi Gras tableau for us to appreciate and remember.

In the 1950s, the area and its surroundings were demolished and replaced by the Civic Center—a development that comprises City Hall, the New Orleans Public Library, and the former residence of the Louisiana Supreme Court. The physical structures are no more. But the music, masking, and parading that traditionally expressed pride in their communal identity, and that enacted a vitality of life that started in the heart of this Black community, continue to permeate New Orleans as a whole. Even today, the brass bands, the Mardi Gras Indians, the Skull and Bones Gangs, and the social and pleasure clubs join the Baby Dolls in preserving our rich legacy.

Keith Weldon Medley

THE
"BaBY DOLLS"

Introduction

A New Orleans Mardi Gras Masking Tradition

Sure they all call me Baby Doll, that's my name. They have
been calling me Baby Doll for a long time.
—*Clara Belle Moore to Robert McKinney, February 9, 1940*

THE POPULAR NEW ORLEANS tradition of dressing up as a Baby
Doll on Carnival Day had its origins around 1912. The Baby Dolls
began as a kind of Carnival club for women who were working
in the dance halls and brothels. These women worked and
lived in what was an unofficial vice district in the heart of New Orleans,
bordering Perdido, Gravier, Basin, and Locust streets, an urban setting
popularly thought of as "rough." It was the neighborhood from which Louis
Armstrong emerged.

While Armstrong is the Perdido and Gravier neighborhood's most
celebrated son, the area was generally rich in expressive arts and vernacular
culture. On Carnival Day friends and neighbors "masked," that is, created
a collective identity and put on a costume that reflected their sense of
themselves. The most famous were the Black Indians of New Orleans.
Much has been written about the masking tradition in general,[1] but little is
known about a particular African American women's tradition that, though
having waned in popularity, has endured in pockets of the city to persist
through a century. The women from the Perdido and Gravier area who
decided to mask one Mardi Gras, imitating little girls with short skirts and
bonnets, were playing with conventional, paradoxical notions of gender.
These wise, worldly women dressed as innocents, embodying the girlish
disguise of the New Woman of the Progressive Era seeking independence
and self-fulfillment. They called themselves the Million Dollar Baby Dolls.

The Million Dollar Baby Dolls actively participated in the entrepreneurial activity of sponsoring dances with live jazz bands in which some women dressed in a variety of Baby Doll attire, while others cross-dressed and appeared in male clothing. They were simultaneously "women who danced the jazz," "women of the jazz," and jazz entrepreneurs.

In time, the practice spread to the mixed-race Creole families in the Seventh Ward and in the Tremé area, a section of the Sixth Ward that borders the French Quarter. Women in these neighborhoods formed social and pleasure clubs to plan their masking for Carnival. These women generally were mothers of large families. Some groups wore short, sexy costumes imitating the Million Dollar Baby Dolls, and some innovated with Baby Doll costumes resembling the toy doll, complete with lollipops, pacifiers, and bottles. These Baby Doll groups were often accompanied by a mock band consisting of the women's husbands, sons, and other family members. By the 1940s, the Baby Doll masking tradition was well established. Women from different parts of the city might mask a few years as Baby Dolls, follow various marching groups on Carnival Day, and then go on to mask in other traditions.

Those following the Million Dollar Baby Doll tradition and those wives and mothers who formed social clubs and paraded as Baby Dolls existed at the same time. There were sexy Baby Dolls (i.e., "babes") that wore curly wigs, sometimes blonde ones, white face paint, hats (such as poke bonnets), short "chippie" style dresses, garters stuffed with money, stockings, or socks and whips or batons to beat back unwanted advances and, second, little-girl Dolls (i.e., "the toy") who wore short satin dresses and accessorized with bonnets, bloomers, baby bottles, pacifiers, lollipops, garters, socks or stockings, and curly wigs. Sometimes groups of maskers wore both types of regalia, as can be seen in a circa 1938 photograph from *Holiday* magazine.

Both Million Dollar Baby Doll and Social and Pleasure Club Baby Doll practices died out as racial integration brought African Americans more opportunities to participate in Carnival. However, there are current revivals of the practice. Merline Kimble and Lois Nelson revived Merline's grandparents' Gold Digger Baby Doll tradition, which they continue to practice in the Tremé. The late Antoinette K-Doe, known for her Mother-in-Law Lounge, also spearheaded such a revival. Resa "Cinnamon Black" Wilson-Bazile masks at most second-line parades and funeral memorials, and on stage and screen. She is well known, and her Tremé Million Dollar Baby Dolls headline the annual Satchmo salute, a second-line parade that is

These photographs were taken by Bradley Smith in 1938, most likely for *Holiday: The American Travel Magazine,* published from 1928 to 1977 as an organ originally of the American Automobile Association. Smith used the photographs with his promotional materials and included this description: "The high spirit of jazz emerges as these self-styled 'Baby Dolls' strut their stuff at the New Orleans Mardi Gras in the late 1930's. Their organization dates back to New Orleans' famed 'Storyville' of the pre–First World War days." Photographs © by Bradley Smith.

Ernie K-Doe Baby Dolls, including Geannie Thomas (*far left*) and Miriam Batiste Reed (*second from left*). They are "under the bridge" on Claiborne Avenue. Photograph by Royce Osborn, used with permission.

Young women Baby Doll maskers from the community organization The Porch, founded in the Seventh Ward in the wake of Hurricane Katrina. Photograph by Charles Chamberlain, used with permission.

The New Orleans Society of Dance's Baby Doll Ladies, parading on Mardi Gras Day in 2010 with the Zulu Social and Pleasure Club. Photograph by Jeffry Dupuis, used courtesy of Millisia White.

part of a festival to honor Louis Armstrong. A younger group, members of the New Orleans Society of Dance's "Baby Doll Ladies," is resurrecting the tradition that was the art of the Million Dollar Baby Dolls—the burlesque dancing (but not nude dancing)—while incorporating Creole and second-line dancing of the Tremé neighborhood Baby Doll groups, along with contemporary bounce. And as recently as Carnival 2010, historian Charles Chamberlain spotted a group of teenagers masking in traditional Baby Doll outfits. They turned out to be young women who were members of The Porch, a cultural organization created in the wake of Katrina in the Seventh Ward. The young men in the organization were learning about the history of the Skeletons and were preparing to mask for Carnival in that costume. The young women wanted to join the masking, and after some convincing of the board members to allow their young women to celebrate this masking tradition, they wore exquisite, hand-made Baby Doll costumes. Some members include Brittany Brastfield and Sjorie Randolph.

The development of jazz is linked with the dances popularized by women like the Million Dollar Baby Dolls. From the socioeconomic positions they occupy, Baby Dolls dance the dances of the times: from the "black bottom," the strutting moves of the cakewalk; the high kicks of the "naked dance"; the so-called "animal dances" such as foxtrot; and all the "shake" numbers from then till now. Today, the Ernie K-Doe Baby Dolls, the revived Gold Digger Baby Dolls, and Cinnamon Black continue the second-line tradition at Carnival and are a presence during street-masking events at a variety of public settings. As a professional dance company, Millisia White's New Orleans Society of Dance's Baby Doll Ladies showcase Creole dance and put it on par with the other music of New Orleans to share with the world through choreographed stage performances and videography.

The common denominator of all Baby Doll groups is the celebration and promotion of the fierce independence of New Orleans's Creole women and their cultural traditions, emphasizing not only dance but costuming, pageantry, beauty, independence, and, above all else, spirituality. The Baby Doll tradition provides a record of one of the first women's street masking practices in the United States. This group has never been studied before—perhaps because, as working-class Black women, they were not taken seriously, or else because of the predominance of male researchers who routinely overlooked the evidence of women's participation in various aspects of the culture. My goal is to create new knowledge and frameworks for the reinterpretation of existing historical documents. This book provides belated recognition of a vital part of our American culture.

1

Gender, Race, and Masking in the Age of Jim Crow

> How to enjoy it [Mardi Gras] best? Most New Orleanians would suggest that you be up early, about eight or so to see Zulu at the New Basin Canal and follow him for a time. . . . For early afternoon masking, the Orleanian will recommend the Canal Street business section. . . . You might try North Claiborne Ave. for the remarkable "Indians"—Negros in ornate and lavish disguise; or the "Baby Dolls"—dark girls of more than good will.
> — *Harnett Kane,* Queen New Orleans: City by the River, *1949*

AT THE TURN OF THE twentieth century, and well before, African Americans in New Orleans were barred by segregation from participating in White Mardi Gras balls and parades. African Americans were confined to servant-class activity in White krewes and clubs. In response, African Americans formed their own Mardi Gras traditions and festivities, which continue to the present day. These include, most notably, the Zulu Social Aid and Pleasure Club, the Black Indians of New Orleans, the Skull and Bones Gangs, and a distinct Carnival music tradition. The Baby Doll masking tradition is a Mardi Gras custom that started around 1912 and was carried out predominantly by African American women, but with participation from men. In 1939, the Million Dollar Baby Dolls were identified as one of the oldest masking groups by the African American–owned newspaper the *Louisiana Weekly*.

Most of what has been documented regarding African American vernacular culture comes from research, interviews, and exhibitions about largely male-dominated art and culture, such as jazz musicians, Black Indians, and the second-line parades of the social and pleasure clubs. Important as these expressive arts are, they have overshadowed the stories of African American women's participation in Carnival.[1]

The colorfully costumed Million Dollar Baby Doll maskers wore short satin dresses, stockings with garters, and bonnets. They were sexy and sometimes raunchy. The Baby Dolls paraded in their neighborhoods, singing bawdy lyrics to vaudeville show tunes and Creole songs, playing tambourines and cowbells, chanting, and dancing. They were fiercely independent in refusing invitations to join male African American masking groups. For example, John Metoyer, a founding member of the Zulu Social Aid and Pleasure Club, asked the Baby Dolls to mask with them, but the women preferred to have their own gang and go their own way. Later in the day, they would eventually follow the Zulu Parade or wind up in the midst of the Black Indians, or with the variously attired members of the Skull and Bones Gangs. If they were not making a scene, Baby Dolls were where the scene was happening.

The Baby Doll practice is reported to have begun in the quasi-legal red-light district, the area of "vice" for African Americans in a section called Back o' Town. It was quasi-legal because the ordinance that established Storyville as the legal red-light district a short distance away also established the Perdido Street area, but then held that section's sanctioning in abeyance. Back o' Town was a back swamp, a low-lying area that separated the city from Lake Pontchartrain and was home to the city's first cemetery. After the Civil War, freed slaves moved into the area, as did immigrants from southern Italy who also left the nearby river plantations. By the turn of the century, Back o' Town was an ethnically mixed community.[2] Despite its reputation, there was more to the Back o' Town area than prostitution and gambling.

Residents raised children in the area, earned a living, and created cultural traditions that have endured. A portion of the section was referred to as the Battlefield, where people would come to show off, settle scores, and enjoy life. Carnival activities that were popular in Back o' Town were repeated in other parts of the city. In the 1920s, even a young Mahalia Jackson left the protection of her neighborhood to venture some distance to Sixth and Willow streets to see the Mardi Gras Indians and perhaps a Baby Doll or two. Mahalia's strict and devout Aunt Duke would have been furious if she had known. Mahalia's biographer explains the allure:

The tribe of Indian Chiefs and Baby Dolls (top-echelon whores)

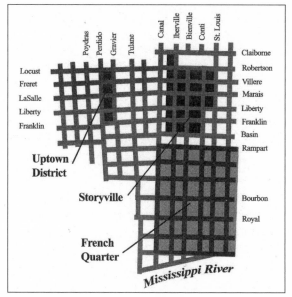

Map by Sam Rykels of vice-district boundaries defined by Ordinance 13485. Reproduced with permission from Alecia Long, *The Great Southern Babylon: Sex, Race, and Respectability in New Orleans, 1865–1920* (Baton Rouge: Louisiana State University Press, 2004).

were widely sought as the most splendid in the City, bar none—the costumes usually scrimped for penny by penny, year-round. The black Zulu parade was topped only by Rex, to white eyes; by none, to black, who on this one day couldn't care less what any white thought. It was Mardi Gras! Masks were encouraged not to come off 'til sundown. The law looked the other way (it couldn't have coped anyway).

As the city blinked awake, its children knew they were unloved if they weren't hurried into costume and painted and put into position early to watch the parades and all the big "Mardi Graws"—strange beings today, mystifying friends and encircling strangers, . . . the air electric, miming made easy as beer and liquor coursed their channels.[3]

Just who were these Baby Dolls, and how did their behavior become famous, even infamous? The difficulties involved in tracking down credible scholarly information have been mind-boggling. Facing a similar problem, Pulitzer Prize–winning historian Stacy Schiff captured the dilemmas involved in writing about women's accomplishments while facing the challenges of male hegemonic practices and discourses. She found the research for her book about the Greek-born Egyptian ruler Cleopatra to be exceptionally challenging.

> Women's lives are very difficult to write about. . . . [I]t's piecing together a life from the tiniest of Mosaic tiles. . . . [B]iography is always puzzle making to some extent; but this was just of the tiniest little pieces. . . . [Y]ou're left with very tendentious sources, with very scant sources. You're reading in the margins, basically, and you're having to somehow read the silences, really, is what it comes down to. . . . I felt I was always . . . walking on egg shells. You're always piecing together things, trying not to jump to a conclusion in any way and, you know, you're reading people like Cicero, who you know are by definition biased. You know, Cicero writing about a foreign woman who's rich and has a better library than he has is not going to give you a particularly objective view of the person in question.[4]

As with Schiff's experience, men have written about the Baby Dolls largely from a decidedly non-feminist stance. Such perspectives have left us with only the most salacious details, emphasizing the titillation of uninhibited sexual display over the collective activities of which these women were so capable. My purpose here is to exemplify the artistic value and to clarify the diverse practices of the masking tradition for the women in Back o' Town as well as to reveal their sociopolitical struggles to realize their own passions, imaginations, historic understandings, and joie de vivre.

THE MILLION DOLLAR BABY DOLLS

The popular picture of the Baby Doll tradition stems from a single source that has been duplicated in the scholarly and tourist literature about New Orleans. The information was collected by Louisiana Writers' Project fieldworker Robert McKinney, an African American journalist whose writings could be found in the African American papers the *Chicago Defender* and the *Louisiana Weekly*. McKinney served as a case manager for the Federal Works Project before joining Lyle Saxon's Louisiana Project in 1935.[5] McKinney's characterization was edited and published in its final form by three White men: Lyle Saxon, Edward Dreyer, and Robert Tallant.[6] There is little evidence that any of these men directly interviewed the Baby Dolls;

they seem to have relied solely on the material collected by McKinney. Mc-Kinney's interviews with a variety of Black New Orleanians were included in the various works edited by Saxon and Tallant, including *Gumbo Ya-Ya: Folktales of Louisiana,* a book still in print and in wide circulation, notably at many tourist spots in Louisiana. The book is in the public domain, allowing the entire contents to be available online. McKinney has never been properly acknowledged for his critical role in reaching African Americans in the Depression, who opened up to him because they trusted him. His interviews and journalism are at the heart of *Gumbo Ya Ya*'s Black folk material.

ROBERT JOSEPH MCKINNEY

What I have been able to piece together is that Robert Joseph McKinney may have been born to Robert McKinney Jr. and Leontine Bartholomew on April 7, 1909. Robert Jr., in turn, was born to Robert McKinney (1850–1922) and Hannah Scott (born 1851) in August 1880 in Louisiana. Robert Jr.'s parents were from Mississippi but had married in Orleans Parish in February 1878. According to the 1900 census, they were renting their home at 2911 South Rampart Street, near the hub of African American commercial districts in the Central City. In 1900 Hannah and Robert had been married twenty-one years. Hannah had given birth to three children, only one of whom was living, and that was Robert Jr. The adults in Robert Jr.'s home performed manual labor. Hannah reported her occupation as cook; Robert Sr. was a laborer. In 1900 Robert Jr. was nineteen years old and could read and write, the only person in his home that could, but he worked as a servant. By 1920, Robert Jr. was living with his parents at 2125 Foucher Street. His parents were working for private families as yardman and cook, and Robert Jr., now thirty-nine, was listed as a hotel porter. By 1940, Robert Jr. was a porter at the Metairie Golf Club and resided at 1907 Fern, where he had lived since at least 1938. Robert Jr. died on January 9, 1958, at the age of seventy.

Leontine Bartholomew married Robert McKinney Jr. on December 17, 1908. The bride was twenty and the groom twenty-eight.[7] Leontine Bartholomew was the daughter of Louis and Alice Bartholomew. At the time of the 1900 census, Leontine was fourteen years old and had an older sister and two younger brothers. The family resided at 7505 Esther Street in the Sixteenth Ward. Her parents had been married sixteen years by then, and all four of her mother's children were living. Leontine's father worked as

a laborer. All children were listed as attending school, and the entire family was literate. Leontine was a 1906 graduate of Leland University with a
Normal and College Preparatory Diploma.[8] Leontine's coursework began
with an elementary school curriculum. She completed Leland's high-school
curriculum to prepare for their teacher-training class. Leontine died on
February 9, 1915, at the age of twenty-seven. Robert Joseph was six.

Robert Joseph attended McDonogh Thirty-five, the first public high
school in New Orleans for African Americans. He was active in co-curricu-
lar pursuits such as writing comic dialogue and selling ads for the yearbook,
The Roneagle. Robert Joseph was president of the 1929 graduating class and
circulation manager of the yearbook. He was one of the directors in the
boy's section of the Decorum Club and a writer for the *Hi Smile* student
newspaper. In 1933 he graduated from Xavier University of Louisiana,
where he had been president of the Athletic Association, business manager
for *The Annual* and the *Herald Newspaper,* and played on the football team.
He was an athletics delegate and a member of the Negro History Club. He
was in the Dramatics Club and in the school orchestra.

Robert Joseph went on to work as a case manager for the Federal Works
Project and then transitioned into the Louisiana Writers' Project in 1935.
Between 1935 and 1938 he wrote articles that appeared in the nationally syn-
dicated African American newspaper the *Chicago Defender* on topics largely
pertaining to New Orleans culture and arts.[9] In working for the Louisiana Writers' Project, he interviewed a wide range of African Americans,
harvesting the folk culture, underworld practices, and spiritual traditions
then flourishing. New Deal historian David Taylor described McKinney's
contribution as having written "the manuscript on black life and canvassed
the restaurants, hotels, and taxi companies that were available to black
residents and visitors."[10]

In 1938, Polk's New Orleans City Directory listed Robert Joseph at a
rooming house run by Mrs. Louise Bartholemew Bonner (ca. 1888–1943)
of 257 Cherokee Street, his maternal aunt. Robert Joseph McKinney may
have died on January 21, 1948, at the age of thirty-nine.[11] Aside from being
mentioned in *Gumbo Ya-Ya,* Robert Joseph was consigned to obscurity
along with the hundreds of anonymous fieldworkers whose community
knowledge was essential in bringing to America awareness of its hidden
cultures. His personal motto selected to accompany his photograph in the
1933 Xavier University yearbook, *The Lighthouse,* was one penned by Oliver

Robert Joseph McKinney, 1933, from
The Lighthouse, the Xavier University
yearbook. Courtesy Xavier University
Archives.

Wendell Holmes in *The Autocrat of the Breakfast Table:* "It is faith in something and enthusiasm for something that makes life worth looking at."

Robert Joseph lived his life accordingly. Because of his keen eye for detail, classical education, work ethic, interpersonal skills, sense of humor,
and belief in the essential dignity of all classes of Black New Orleanians,
we are left with an invaluable record of the ordinary and extraordinary customs lived out by a cross-section of the city's citizens, traditions continued
to the present day by their descendants.

WHO WERE THE MILLION DOLLAR BABY DOLLS?

The Million Dollar Baby Dolls were women who paraded on the street together wearing short pleated skirts, bloomers with ruffles and bows, waists
or halters, poke bonnets, and socks or stockings held up by garters for se-
curing dollar bills. They donned wigs of corkscrew curls in various colors,
including blonde, and they made extensive use of makeup. Their dresses

were made of pink or blue satin to achieve the goal of looking as innocent as possible.

Dressing up as Baby Dolls was reported to have begun when a group of uptown (that is, above Canal Street) prostitutes decided to show up a group of downtown (below Canal Street) prostitutes on Mardi Gras. Each woman had to put up her own money to make her costume, including "green money" overflowing from the garter belt that rested snugly on her thigh. During Carnival, these women smoked cigars, flung money at men, and challenged other groups of masked "sportin'" women. They were known for "walking raddy" (a kind of strut that would end with the steps needed to "shake on down"), "shake dancing," singing traditional Creole songs and blues, turning tricks, drinking, smoking reefers, and "starting and causing" street fights complete with brick throwing and razor flashing. The name they adopted for themselves, "Baby Dolls," was based on what their pimps called them. Like the Mardi Gras Indians, they "masked" twice a year: on Carnival and on St. Joseph's Night, March 19.

Rounding out popular descriptions of the Million Dollar Baby Dolls are accounts primarily from male musicians. Coming from the dance halls and brothels, the Million Dollar Baby Dolls specialized in "the naked dance," which Ferdinand "Jelly Roll Morton" LaMothe believed was an art form in the city's brothels.[12] Jazz musician and New Orleans native George "Creole" Guesnon recounted the scene on St. Joseph Night at the Humming Bird Cabaret on Bienville and Marais streets in 1927: "What I saw there I ain't never saw before. It was the Baby Dolls . . . kicking high their pretty legs in the fancy lace stockings, filled with fifty and one hundred dollar bills."[13] Robert Tallant described their activities at the Zulu Mardi Gras parade in 1947, in which one Baby Doll "began doing a shake number. She accomplished what is called 'going all the way down,' lowering herself to the ground, shaking violently all the time, until she was stretched out on her back, resting upon her shoulders and feet, with hips gyrating violently and her breasts quivering like jelly under her pink satin halter she wore above her brief skirt."[14]

Baby Dolls gained a reputation as agile dancers, sharp entrepreneurs in the sex work industry, and as tough women. The noted New Orleans chef Austin Leslie, who was born in 1934 and as a child probably saw the Baby Dolls in their heyday, described their dress and demeanor: "all those women dressed like little babies, in hot pink and sky blue. You fool with them, they'd cut you too."[15] Beatrice Hill was one of the tough ones. She recalls, "We had stacks of dollars in our stockings and in our hands. We went to the Sam Bonart playground on Rampart and Poydras and bucked up against each other to see who had the most money,"[16] though admittedly, they made peace with one another. In a rather reductive portrayal of a complex sociopolitical artistic expression, historian Samuel Kinser compared them to the Mardi Gras Indian gangs that were "led by a fighter, usually a murderous one."[17]

A different perspective on the female tradition of the Baby Dolls is offered by jazz musician Eddie "Duke" Edwards, whose aunt, Vanilla, was a Baby Doll.[18] The Edwards family lives in Edgard, in St. John the Baptist Parish. Many of the women who were Baby Dolls came to New Orleans from the river parishes. "Out here you are somebody's daughter, and somebody's niece. In the river parishes, people's behavior was governed by the 'Society.' Crimes against women such as domestic violence would be handled by the woman's relatives." No such protections existed in the city for these women; so they relied on the survival spirit they inherited from their families. This spirit of independence and defiance grew in reaction to the conditions African American women faced at the bottom of the gender, race, class, and caste system in New Orleans. By 1912 Blacks' legal and social second-class citizenship had finally gained the upper hand in what had formerly been a more integrated city.

"BEFORE WE WERE BABY DOLLS"

Robert Tallant thought of opening the chapter on African American Carnival traditions in *Gumbo Ya-Ya* as follows: "Every night is like Saturday night in Perdido Street, wild and fast and hot with sin. But the night before Mardi Gras blazed to a new height as the denizens of that vicinity refused to wait the hours that stretched before tomorrow and rode them through the night as if they were bucking, fiery steeds come to life on a madly whirling carousel."

But the sentence sensationalizing behaviors as "wild" was scratched out, and the paragraph started at "as the denizens." Also scratched out in an edited version was the chapter's subtitle, penciled in as "Nigger Mardi Gras." What Tallant did not ask was why these people (musicians, sex workers, cooks, laundresses, storekeepers, barbers, hair dressers, bar owners, etc.)

acted as if every night was like Saturday night. What turned these inhabitants into "bucking, fiery steeds"? What "madly whirling carousel" has forced them to "come to life," that is, to have to come to *this life* in the District?[19] What is striking is the way Tallant begins the chapter as if he dropped into a scene that has no social or historical context. He characterizes its inhabitants as being in a state of perpetual play, as if these people are not fully and completely engaged in an industry, i.e., the business of producing pleasure for others. But the editors can act as if all this were mere spectacle, not only because of their White, male, and class privilege. Lyle Saxon made it clear that of the ethnic communities presented in *Gumbo Ya-Ya,* the Creoles—who for him were racially White, never having "colored blood"—were on top and the Baby Dolls were on the bottom of the social hierarchy. Saxon believed that "Creoles [were] the top of the heap," compared to those at the other extreme, "such as Negro prostitutes parading on Mardi Gras."[20] In addition, it is not clear whether Saxon and Tallant ever set foot on the Baby Dolls' streets, nor whether they interviewed any of the so-called denizens. To get their information, they literally copied from the reports of Robert McKinney. Many of McKinney's transcripts of interviews with the members of the Zulu Club and the Baby Dolls were marked "Private" and slated for Tallant's files.

To complicate matters further, there are few sources in which the voices of Black women who lived in the District can be heard. Police records, travelogues, sensational descriptions in books and newspapers, and memoirs of male jazz musicians are all that can be mined. The Black women who lived or worked in the District and its surrounding areas were engaged in a variety of occupations, the majority perhaps as sex workers, but also as servants, cooks, seamstresses, and accomplished musicians.[21] They were often single women supporting children, parents, and other relatives through their work. These women are rarely called by their given names. Instead, in numerous sources they are referred to by the epithet of "whore." Jazz musician and writer Danny Barker categorized Black sex workers as "stray whores" (who were associated with drugs, alcohol abuse, ignorance, uncleanliness, fighting, and jail), seemingly the majority of women, with the more rare, so-called "first-class whores" (or "sporting women," who were intelligent, drug free, and particular about their associates).[22]

The historical record tells us little about these women and what they did to keep their spirits up in the face of daily humiliations. A recent exhibi-

Virginia Green, age eighteen, 1912. Louisiana Division/City Archives, New Orleans Public Library.

Louisa Barnes, age twenty-two, 1912. Louisiana Division/City Archives, New Orleans Public Library.

Bertha Bailey, age twenty-eight, 1912. Louisiana Division/City Archives, New Orleans Public Library.

tion of photographs, "Hidden from History: Unknown New Orleanians," from the New Orleans Public Library brings their vulnerability and entrepreneurial determination to life. "Even though the Storyville ordinance ostensibly made prostitution legal within the District's boundaries, women were frequently arrested for petty theft and pick-pocketing, drunkenness, disorderly behavior, fighting, reviling the police and other such crimes. In spite of the District's reputation for swinging good times, and the romanticization of prostitution in New Orleans," the photographs of Virginia Green, Louisa Barnes, and Bertha Bailey, as with other women labeled as prostitutes during this period, "indicate that for most women, prostitution was neither glamorous nor easy."[23]

Storyville, a portion of the city set aside by an 1897 ordinance legalizing prostitution, gambling, and other "vices," was segmented into two areas, supposedly one White and the other Black. Black women worked in both sections. The corralling of black-market businesses into one easily accessible area allowed for the development of a robust financial industry, connected as it was with rail lines and in close proximity to the city's business district.

These women lived in Storyville proper, not in the uptown vice district some blocks away, and had many run-ins with the law. On April 29, 1912, twenty-eight-year-old Bertha Bailey was arrested as "a suspicious thief." She also resided near Virginia Green and Louisa Barnes, according to police records of her at 415 N. Liberty (currently Tremé) Street.[24] Twenty-two-year-old Louisa Barnes was arrested on May 23, 1912. Accused of being a "sneak thief," she served ten days in Parish Prison. She purportedly resided at 515 Bienville Street. Virginia Green was just eighteen when she was arrested and charged with "larceny from the person"[25] (i.e., pickpocketing) on November 29, 1912. A petite, brown-skinned young woman who reported her address as 1402 Bienville Street, she was already labeled a "prostitute" on her Bertillon card, a record-keeping system then used by police. Later she was arrested with unnamed "others" for "operating an immoral house" and for "grand larceny." The dispositions of her cases are unknown since these were not recorded in the Orleans Parish Criminal Courts' Criminal Defendants' Index.

Bertha, Louisa, and Virginia were busily occupied earning a living (whether as sex workers, vendors, hustlers, performers, seamstresses, or servants) and trying to survive in what might have been the toughest environment Black women had encountered since enslavement. By 1912, New Orleans was firmly in the grip of legal segregation. Beginning with the outlawing of interracial marriage in 1894, federal legislation separating Black and White seating on trains and all public accommodations in 1896 (*Plessy v. Ferguson*),[26] disenfranchisement of Blacks by the state constitutional convention in 1898, segregation on streetcars in 1902 (the Separate Street Car Law), and the 1908 outlawing of concubinage, social attitudes and practices hardened to extend segregation to residential areas, saloons, circuses and tent entertainment, sporting events, and jails and prisons.[27] No area of life was left unaffected. Even in Storyville the color line persisted. The city ordinance issued in 1897 stipulated that Black and White women were not allowed to reside or work in the same house, though they could occupy adjacent buildings.[28]

In 1910, Black women made up 28 percent of those working as prostitutes in Storyville, according to Craig Foster. Darker-skinned Black women labored in poorer conditions and earned less income than did light-skinned Black women, who more often worked in "high-class" bordellos.

> The lowest type of brothel was the crib. The women who worked in the crib were considered the lowest caliber and, consequently, lived the most miserable lives. They were usually black and catered to other blacks or to the lower classes. The cribs themselves consisted of a small room attached to an even smaller room or entry hall separated by a wall or curtain. The spartan furnishings consisted of a bed (or a mattress on the floor), a chair, and a washstand. These rooms were open around the clock and were used by several prostitutes working in shifts.
>
> . . . The differences between the cribs and the high-class parlor houses were emphasized by unwritten rules of segregation. The parlor houses and cribs that were located south of Liberty Street were white clientele only, consequently commanding higher prices. The houses and cribs between Liberty and Villere streets were occupied and frequented by both races. The section between Villere and Robertson streets was the black section. This area charged the lowest prices, had the roughest clientele, and had numerous street walkers doing back alley trade.[29]

For Black women in the area of Perdido and Gravier streets, life was equally difficult, if not more so. McKinney records the nature of the women's working conditions with astounding candor. Whereas men played board games like checkers and cards and wore expensive clothes, "their" women hustled customers into little dank rooms for sex. The men kept enough money on them (their bankroll) to bail "their" women out of jail when the need would arise. Some women, like Beatrice Hill, maintained their own houses and charged other women for room use. The women walked the streets in "short tight skirts" with a "fascinating vigor," as if "the rhythm of their movement was the key to their success." McKinney wrote that the women dance, "sing 'low down' songs, use profanity with aplomb, flip their hair with indifference." They did not need to dodge the police because they paid a regular graft to them and personally knew the officials. Some, like McKinney's interviewee, Clara Belle Moore, grew in leadership ability to become the virtual "boss of the neighborhood," meaning these women's capacity to command respect was evident in spite of the turbulence of their lives. McKinney did not miss the fact that these were "hard working women." And, he adds with special emphasis, "They are proud."

And they were defiant. When insulted, Clara Belle recalled that the Baby Dolls' retort would be, "Kiss our tails, cause the babies and the dolls don't give a damn." They were "raddy" women who did not care about what others who devalued them thought of them.

These women made an impression on Louis Armstrong, who provides one of the few eyewitness accounts of everyday life, his own life.

> I had been brought up around honky-tonks on Liberty and Perdido where life was just about the same as it was in Storyville except that the chippies were cheaper. The gals in my neighborhood did not stand in cribs wearing their fine silk lingerie as they did in Storyville. They wore silk lingerie just the same but under their regular clothes. Our hustlers sat on their steps and called on to "Johns" as they passed by. They had to keep an eye on the cops all the time. . . .
>
> When the girls were hustling they would wear real short dresses and the very best silk stockings to show off their fine, big legs.[30]

To be sure, if life for higher-caste Black Creole women in New Orleans was difficult, for working-class Black women, having a job that did not involve the risk of sexual exploitation was rare. For the women under discussion here, life was exceptionally difficult. Crushing poverty, poor health, illiteracy, unsanitary living conditions, venereal disease, unchecked drug and alcohol addiction, and criminal activity from murder to robbery and fighting—hence regular encounters with the criminal justice system—had all become a normalized part of their existence.

Judging from the advertisements in Blue Books (published directories of names and addresses of prostitutes in the District), some light-skinned Black women, such as Emma Sears, who associated with the well-appointed brothel of Lulu White—herself a fair-skinned Black woman—could express their creative talents in music they wrote and performed. Lulu White gained control of the representation of herself and her female employees by insisting on defining them using the existing color caste system, which distinguished Blacks along the lines of skin tone. With lighter skin having been exploited as desirable in the local guidebooks, Lulu White advertised her sex workers as octoroons. But for dark-skinned Black women, in addition to their gender and class status, their skin tone further truncated even their creative opportunities. What then could they do to keep their spirits up? Like other aggrieved groups, they appropriated Mardi Gras for their own purposes.

For maskers, Mardi Gras is more than a day. It is a workspace in which one prepares to participate in the concrete transgression of the everyday social order, to perform reversals, to participate in communal activity, to forge collective identities, and to assert one's personhood. Carnival identities are in existence all year long, but normally submerged in daily life. Roger Abrahams's analysis of such activities on the island of St. Vincent demonstrates that "rude" behaviors (such as drinking, verbal and physical play, or "nonsense" activities) are given the greatest freedom of expression on Carnival. These behaviors are practiced all year long largely by men who are "sporty," constituting the reputations of men who exist outside the female-dominated yard or household and are thought to be a direct attack on notions of respectability, namely family mores and customs. Abrahams observes that the rude behaviors contain their own social values. It is on Carnival that conflicting lifestyles and competing value systems are expressed. Sporty people harness the festival's "energies by embodying these otherwise embarrassing nonhousehold 'nonsense' behaviors in their licentious festival performances."[31] Similarly, the Baby Dolls took their everyday, ordinary identities and marked the city's environs with their stamp of performativity. They journeyed from place to place on Carnival Day: singing the blues, dancing, smoking cigars, earning money and flaunting it in an abundant display in their garters, challenging other groups of women with how "sharp" they looked in their little "chippy" outfits.

"LET EVERY TUB STAND ON ITS OWN BOTTOM":
THE ORIGINS OF THE MILLION DOLLAR BABY DOLLS

After a long night at work, and after hearing the "buzz" around how the downtown Black sportin' women were planning to mask for the upcoming Carnival season, Beatrice Hill made a decision. It was time for the uptown women to make a statement. Only part of what happened next is widely quoted; the rest of the story has not been quoted or referenced at all. According to Beatrice Hill, "Here is what happened in 1912. Ida Jackson, Millie Barnes and Sallie Gail and a few other downtown gals was making up to mask on Mardi Gras." Beatrice did not know the particulars, but she wanted to form a group of her friends and colleagues. "Well, I wasn't good at forming no club or nothing like that, so I told Leola Tate." Once Leola understood Beatrice's desires and concerns, Leola called the women together in the wee hours of the morning, "about three thirty after they had finished work." The women met at Beatrice's home and Leola set the rules. "We wouldn't do no drinking because we wanted to talk sense and get something done."

Beatrice held Leola in high esteem. Leola had been active in many church and social aid and pleasure clubs and knew how to organize groups and activities. According to Beatrice, "Leola and all of us was sitting around the room. The room was packed. Leola who used to belong to church and one of the helping hands associations and who use to go to all those meetings and things, says, 'Let's come to order.' She stands up and says, what's your pleasure? We didn't have none but we had a motion and an object. I raised that by saying we wanted to mask up in an association for Mardi Gras to outdo all [Black women][32] maskers."

In 1912 the idea of a grown woman as a Baby Doll was a titillating image to arouse men's sexual desire, and the women were poised to use that image strategically. When it came to selecting a name for their association, Althea Brown is reported to have said, "Let's be ourselves, let's be Baby Dolls, that's what the pimps call us." According to Beatrice, "that suited everybody." To this group of extraordinarily independent women, and calculating and defiant ones at that, Althea's suggestion was packed with their experiences in sex work.

As Beatrice continues her story, the women in the room began to pull out their money. The social aid and benevolent societies of the day charged each member dues, and the money was pooled and used for the

Baby Dolls dancing in the streets, Mardi Gras, 1931. These recently discovered photos are taken from an unidentified film shot about 1931, according to Story Sloane of Sloane Gallery. Used with permission from The Sloane Collection/www.SloaneGallery.com.

"Baby Dolls posing for camera." Baby Doll celebration on Mardi Gras Day in New Orleans, 1942. From the Collection of the U.S. Works Progress Administration of Louisiana, courtesy State Library of Louisiana.

association's activities and responsibilities. Knowing this, the women began to contribute their money. Leola Tate stopped them in their tracks and ordered the group to "Hold your horses. Let every tub stand on its own bottom." This common phrase has always meant for each person to contribute her own share and not let a few handle the burden for the whole. It meant that each should make her own preparations as if she were relying solely on herself and judged according to her own merits. Then someone asked about naming their group and, stressing their financial success, the women decided to call themselves the "'Million Dollar Baby Dolls' and be red hot."

At minimum each woman had to mask with a stocking containing at least fifty dollars. Not only were they "red hot," but they determined to be independent of the male-dominated masking groups like the Indians and the Zulus. "We didn't have nothing to do with the Zulus," said Beatrice. "Old Johnny Metoyer wanted us to come along with them but we wouldn't do it. We told Johnny we were out to do up some fun in our own way and we were stopping at nothing, no indeed. Yes sir, the Zulus had their gang and we had ours."

When Robert McKinney interviewed Clara Belle Moore in February 1940, she labeled herself a "Baby Doll today and every day." She recalled that, when she was just twenty years old, a gathering of women decided on a collective identity to imitate Clara Belle's regular Carnival costume, consisting of a tight skirt, bloomers, and a rimmed hat. They wore "short gingham red plaid dresses" that hung from a yoke. The Baby Dolls wore "little bonnets and curls and bloomers," yet some could be seen in "long-waisted dresses with a short, pleated skirt."

According to a traditional saying in New Orleans, "You could do what you wanted to do on Mardi Gras." And so many women did. Clara Belle noted that these women would meet at someone's home to put on their outfits. "This was done because a lot of our husbands and old-men didn't want us to be Baby Dolls cause they knew a lot of men would follow us on the street and try to make mashes [i.e. have sex] on us. We didn't tell them how we were going to mask but just came out as a Baby Doll on Mardi Gras. And boy was we tight!" Beatrice Hill told McKinney that their initial outfits consisted of rainbow colors, with panel backs and fronts made out of gold lace. Some of the women made their own costumes, and some had them made. Money was key to the costume to showcase their economic prowess. Each of the women with Beatrice had at least fifty dollars in her stockings. The garter on the thigh with money has come to be a signature component of the masking tradition. On that first outing, there were about thirty women with "money all over them" and "even in our bloomers."

Needless to say, such showmanship attracted a large following. Beatrice was thrilled that the men "liked the way we shook our [bottoms], and we shook it like we wanted to." Starting at 10:15 in the morning, they paraded around parts of the city. Then they met up at Sam Bonart Playground "on Rampart and Poydras and bucked against each other to see who had the most money. Leola had the most, one hundred and two dollars. I had ninety-six dollars and I was second, but I had money at home in case I ran out."

The Million Dollar Baby Dolls transgressed the socially constructed hierarchy and went downtown to directly challenge the other Black women maskers on their own turf. Beatrice recalled with pride, "We went downtown and talking about putting on the ritz, we showed them [women] how to put on the ritz. Boy we was smoking cigars and flinging ten and twenty dollar bills through the air." The response of the downtown women in Beatrice's view was concession. "The gals couldn't do nothing but look at us. They had to admit that we were stuff." Of course the flagrant display of flashing and tossing away money made a scene. "When we started pitching dollars around we had sportin' [Black men] falling on their faces trying to get that money." The uptown-downtown rivalry was short lived. As Beatrice noted, "We all made peace."

For the Million Dollar Baby Dolls, the masking was not just a one-day event but a way of life and a stage act designed for their economic profit, even if that stage was on the street. A second day for Black Carnival revelers to mask was the night of the feast of St. Joseph, an annual event on March 19. Sicilian Americans introduced the practice of building elaborate food altars on the day of the saint's annual feast. When they immigrated to New Orleans and its surroundings in massive numbers at the turn of the century, they kept the tradition alive. African American Spiritual churches were quick to integrate this practice into their own altar-making rotations of commemoration of saints and other biblical figures. There was much synergy between these ethnic groups as Italian Americans were known to attend the services at Spiritual churches.[33] The pageantry of St. Joseph's Day resonated with this African American collective thanksgiving and created an evening ritual involving masking, chanting, and parading through the streets. In fact, night masking on St. Joseph's feast night had become just as important to the Mardi Gras Indian community as Carnival Day.

The Million Dollar Baby Dolls were among those who celebrated on St. Joseph's night.[34] Robert McKinney noted, "This is the night that is a second Mardi Gras for a lot of people, i.e., the Baby Dolls and their ilk. They mask and wave their hips, sing low down blues songs to the accompaniment of loud cornets, banjos, drums and other instruments. They frolic on the streets in the same manner as they do on Fat Tuesday; their shimmies are strictly 'solid' and always attract a large crowd."

As the Million Dollar Baby Doll association grew and matured, they held significant social events in the community and became a real presence. They did not simply parade on Carnival Day. They hired bands and held dances. Beatrice describes the band that the Baby Dolls hired as consisting of a cornetist, a flautist, a drummer, a banjoist, a bassist, and a few others. She praised their musical performance because, when the band's music "heated," it allowed the Baby Dolls to "strut," to shake it on down while dancing.

Financial and personal independence as both a style of life and an attitude for these women is verified by Beatrice: "We on down the years never did ask any help from anybody." In 1914, however, the Million Dollar Baby Dolls were hired by a local distributor of the Bernheim Distillery to advertise I. W. Harper whiskey.[35] A sampling of Bernheim's I. W. Harper trade cards used to advertise their products from 1900 onward confirms the company's use of Black and female bodies to appeal to their multi-racial and predominately male clientele.[36] Harper was also a popular brand among the New Orleans Jazz Age community.[37]

Eventually, this group of Baby Dolls gave way to the natural aging process and its vicissitudes. Beatrice's story comes to a close with the words, "We couldn't keep up our association. Some of us got sick, some of them dropped out, but the Million Dollar Baby Dolls went on."

AND THE TUBS STOOD

During the 1912 Mardi Gras, a group of women who lived and worked uptown were deliberating over how to respond to the costuming plans of a rival group of downtown women. Uptowner Althea Brown is credited with having the vision for her friends to "be themselves," that is, to be Baby Dolls.[38] As downtown residents, Virginia, Bertha, and Louisa might have encountered the uptown women who decided to mask as Baby Dolls and who called themselves the "Million Dollar Baby Dolls."[39] The aim of their masking was to gain recognition from the only people who would see them as human beings, that is, other Black women in the sex industry. The Baby Doll tradition evolved out of need for more than a costume. It was a ritual of recognition. Even though the groups were rivals, they could offer each other validation in a way that was impossible to achieve with the majority of middle-class Americans, Black or White, male or female, rich or poor.

Largely objectified and denigrated by Whites and men and middle- and upper-class African Americans, with each other these Black women could experience the pleasure of mutual recognition. That is, they could see each other as separate subjects with "equivalent centers of experience."[40] Mutual recognition is the development of the capacity to have an emotional identification with the perspective of another person even if the two do not agree. The Baby Doll masking tradition served as a form of play that built relational bonds among similarly situated Black women. In the safety of play, the uptown women knew that the downtown women would recognize and respond to their statement of "I am." "I am alive." "I am myself."[41] "I am a Baby Doll!"

Women Dancing the Jazz

Early New Orleans' musicians did not call their music Jazz, they called it
Ragtime. This implied a syncopated treatment or a rag in time on marches
and other popular music of the day to induce people to dance.

—*Old U.S. Mint display*

• •

T HE TIES BETWEEN the Million Dollar Baby Dolls and jazz
musicians is complex, and much of this relationship remains
unknown. What is known, however, is that these were women
who "danced the jazz."[1] They improvised movements to the new
rhythms and defined their lives through and around this music. As such,
they helped to shape the development of jazz itself.

In the second decade of the twentieth century, New Orleans jazz musicians advertised the places where they were to perform by riding around
neighborhoods in wagons and trucks, playing their tunes. Frequently they
would encounter each other on street corners. If they were rivals, they
might engage each other in battles to claim musical superiority. These
impromptu street-corner competitions were called "bucking" or "cutting"
contests.

One such contest occurred between an esteemed band leader, Henry
"Kid" Rena (pronounced *Ruh-nay*) and noted trumpeter Lee Collins before
or around the 1920s. Their contest occurred, according to Collins, while
Kid Rena was advertising for a dance to be given by the Lady Baby Dolls.[2]
Beatrice Hill describes the early promotion of the Baby Doll dances: "Leola
went out and got a band. We had to pay two fifty a piece for that. She had
got sign carriers. We had to pay half a dollar a piece for that. That's all the

public expense I think we had. There must have been more but Leola took care of that. We gave her the money."[3]

In New Orleans, African American dance and music have a symbiotic relationship. Historically, the musicians have changed their rhythms to fit the dance steps of the time. And those people who frequented the dance halls and honky-tonks, like the Million Dollar Baby Dolls, made the ever-changing dance steps. In 1912, the steps were "hot,"[4] and the music accommodated.[5] Noted jazz musician and historian Danny Barker makes this point repeatedly in a 1992 interview. Barker recalled watching a performance of Kid Rena: "Kid Rena opened his shirt like [sound of buttons popping], sit on stage back of that horn, never went in the high register of the horn. Just played pretty music. . . . You don't get winded. A man'll get on the floor and dance with a woman if it ain't too exciting, because . . . their hearts can be beating together, and their foots shoving, and knees hitting against one another, and belly buttons hitting next to one another. That's what music is all about. A dance."

Writing about the development of jazz in the twentieth century, musicologist Lawrence Gushee noted that "at the outset and for decades to follow jazz was functionally music for dancing."[6] African Americans in the dance halls and honky-tonks were engaging in sexy, expressive, free-spirited dancing to the newly emerging "ratty," or "hot," music. Black New Orleanians took this one step further. They danced in the streets. New Orleans is famous for its parades of live bands and the followers who dance to their music on public thoroughfares. The first line is the band, and the second is the crowd. Reid Mitchell noted that the people who accompanied the bands on the streets, the second line, also helped to shape jazz. "It was the second line that insisted that jazz be played in the streets." Second liners did not want to march—that is, do the old dance steps—they wanted to "jump,"[7] meaning to dance sexy. Danny Barker described the women merrymakers at the bucking contests derisively as "dancing their vulgar dances all through the battle."[8] Despite the disapproval inherent in this statement, he at least etches these women into the historical record as women "dancing the jazz."

JAZZ AS MUSIC FOR DANCING

That American hot jazz evolved from the dance, the mother of all arts, should be self-evident. However, in these days of commercial

jazz, in which the true dance music is often disguised . . . one is apt
to forget that jazz roots are deeply imbedded in folk arts and the
dance.

    —William Russell, "Jazz Sources," *Dance Observer*, 1940

The beginning of jazz was about producing music that people wanted to
move their bodies to. In the darkened halls, they could experience one another's bodies through dancing sensually to music. It was through their
participation in jazz circles that they could bring their changing social identities away from Victorian-era constriction and into a contemporary view.
The dancers demanded a musical style that matched their feelings, and
they wanted to experience that feeling through their bodies. They wanted
to dance to performances by musicians known for their prowess in delivering "hot," sexy, spontaneous rhythms. If the musicians wanted to get hired
again, they needed to provide the right rhythms.

The early jazz musicians were influenced by the musical genres of
their times: ragtime, gospel, blues, marches. It is widely acknowledged
that a young African American uptowner named Buddy Bolden broke
with traditional dance-music arrangements and introduced to dance-hall
performances versions of established tunes that were syncopated and improvised—in other words, "raggy"[9] music. His transformation of standard
popular tunes and marches of the day was accomplished by quickening
the music's tempo and by incorporating Black church music, syncopation,
improvisation, and the blues. Bolden emerged as a leader among the musicians playing in the new genre. Others followed his lead, and those bands
playing in this ragging style drew large crowds for their dances. A new
music full of energy and fun, well suited to the tastes of young people, had
been born.

One of the favorite songs of early jazz dancers was the "Funky Butt"[10]
(later recorded by Ferdinand "Jelly Roll Morton" LaMothe as "Buddy
Bolden's Blues"). So popular was the song and accompanying dance, the
"funkybuttin',"[11] that many such dances held at the Union Sons Hall on
1319 Perdido resulted in the hall being dubbed the Funky Butt Hall. The
funkybuttin' dance craze spread throughout the South in African American
dance halls, juke joints, and barrel houses. Coot Grant, a performer in the
husband-wife team of Coot Grant and Sox Wilson, though not a New Orleanian, described the "funkybuttin'" dance she saw as a child in Alabama in
the 1910s: "women sometimes pulled up their dresses to show their pretty

petticoats—fine linen with crocheted edges—and that is what happened in the Funky Butt.... I remember a powerful woman who worked in the mills pulling coke from a furnace, a man's job.... When Sue arrived ... people would yell, 'Here come Big Sue! Do the Funky Butt, Baby!' As soon as she got high and happy, she'd ... pull ... up her skirts and grind ... her rear end like an alligator crawling up a bank."[12] The repertoires of early jazz bands included the standard fare of schottisches, waltzes, polkas, mazurkas, and quadrilles. To these they incorporated fast one-steps, slow drags, and blues. The most popular songs were risqué, like "If You Don't Shake You Get No Cake." Also popular were such blues songs as "Make Me a Pallet on the Floor."[13]

Jazz music observers of the time also noted this preference for a few favorite blues and tunes. Quoting a 1911 writer, Gushee highlighted the heart of jazz dance activity to be at Customhouse Street (now Iberville Street) and Franklin Street in the District. The musicians were Black and "often repeated the same selection, but never played it the same way twice."[14] The dances accompanying the music, the writer reported, were a "siege" of erotic ones: "the Grizzly Bear," "Turkey Trot," "Texas Tommy," and "Todolo."

Even as New Orleans's residents left the South to head for points north and west in search of better-paying jobs and to escape the stranglehold of Jim Crow segregation, they continued to make demands on the jazz musicians who entertained them in these new haunts. One type of song that was required was a slow tune to allow dancers to perform the slow drag. Coot Grant described this popular dance most famously: "couples hold on to each other and just grind back and forth in one spot all night."[15]

Danny Barker described a night he performed in Chicago at Warwick Hall, a place known as a gathering spot for Black people from New Orleans, including Louis Armstrong. There they would come together, bring the cuisine of their original region, mingle with the "fast-living" people, and shed work identities. In those new milieus, they could express their submerged identities. Barker felt compelled to play a steady rhythm of swing for the dancers at Warwick Hall, explaining, "People go to a club. If you play the tempo too fast, they gonna walk off the floor, because they didn't come here for no marathon or no Olympics."[16]

By 1932, jazz was firmly established as dance music. The power of the dancers to determine the music can be seen in Barker's recollection of New Orleans native King Oliver's jazz band during their first performance at the Savoy in Harlem, the stronghold of Lindy-hoppers: "They didn't know the tempos of the Savoy, which was the Lindy-hoppers place. They would dance. If you didn't play their tempos, they just look at you. That's where Chick Webb and King Oliver had this battle. . . . They had the truck go around, like I tell in my book. The truck used to go around playing the music, advertising the Savoy. . . . First set, King Oliver played. The second set, nobody danced. They looked. They didn't say nothing. A little jive applause. Then Chick Webb come in, and announce Chick Webb. Big applause. Chick went on and went through that tempo. . . . Start that Lindy-hop. That was them people's rhythm."

"NEW ORLEANS JAZZ WOMEN"

Sherrie Tucker has provided one of the most comprehensive assessments of women's participation in New Orleans jazz. Tucker identified "New Orleans jazz women" as "women who contributed to New Orleans jazz history whether or not they lived in New Orleans." They included musicians and others, "such as garden party entrepreneur Betsy Cole, religious figures such as Mother Catherine Seales, and jazz fans, jazz club members and revivalists such as Myra Menville." She also included "educators, church musicians, musicians who worked with jazz musicians, or who were influenced by jazz."

By this time African American vernacular dance in New Orleans had consolidated into a distinguished style infused by centuries of African dance, religious dances, burlesque dances, second-line dances, jazz dances, and other social dances such as the cakewalk and animal dances. When District-related Baby Dolls paraded on Carnival, they would walk "raddy," stopping periodically to "shake dance."

If female musicians were left out of the histories of jazz, women who contributed to the music by their dancing were likewise ignored by those writing the historical narrative.[17] Tucker noted that "women participated on every instrument, in every genre, in every period of jazz history. We also know that they often participated differently, or in different areas, than ordinarily considered historically important, such as in family bands, all-woman bands, or as dancers or teachers, and that those areas typically became minimized in jazz histories."[18] Tucker offered a further explanation that "often times, as in other areas of social life, women did not have access to roles that historians are accustomed to using in the criterion for historical importance." Tucker's effort is to broaden the scope of jazz activity beyond its traditional bounds, to find "ways to re-frame jazz history so that gender and women are visible."[19] "The study of women in New Orleans jazz history makes it possible not only to locate women in New Orleans jazz as we know it, but to increase our knowledge of both women and men in entire areas of jazz history that have been historically devalued. These include church musicians, vocalists, music education, theatrical performance, dancers and 'all-girl' bands."[20]

One of the best-known jazz dancers was Neliska "Baby" Briscoe. Born in the Tremé, Briscoe started her career as a young child in a local gambling house and cabaret called the Alley on Claiborne and St. Bernard avenues. In 1925, when Neliska was eleven, she sang and entertained with a jazz band consisting of Maurice Dumond, "Big Eye" Louis Nelson, George Henderson, and Odette Davis. According to Debra Mouton, Neliska's daughter, her mother did not seem to have any known connection to any of the Baby Doll groups.[21] Yet Neliska performed regularly at the Entertainer, a club on Franklin Avenue near Customhouse/Iberville that was a frequent haunt of the Million Dollar Baby Dolls. She also performed with Kid Rena and His Hot Eight band for dances at the Astoria. Neliska acquired the nickname "Baby" from her time as a child entertainer, and not in relationship to the masking tradition; nevertheless, this dancer and the Million Dollar Baby Dolls inhabited the same landscape.

"WALKING RADDY"

Classically trained musicians who played established marches and cultured tunes disapproved of the changes to the music, calling this new vernacular "ratty" or "honky-tonk." The slang word "ratty" (also spelled "raddy" in the scholarly literature on jazz and in tourist accounts) came to define a style of music, a kind of "strutting walk," as well as the type of people who enjoyed it. Danny Barker noted that the distinction between "raddy" and "ratty" was a major one in that "ratty" referred to criminal and illegal behavior,[22] whereas "raddy" referred to "not giving a damn" about what others thought about one's behavior, art, and way of life.

When they became the Million Dollar Baby Dolls, Beatrice Hill recalled that, at Carnival, "we went to the Sam Bonart playground on Poydras Street and bucked each other to see who had the most money."[23] Bonart attended public schools and would go on to establish a successful store at the corner of South Rampart and Poydras streets. Before they were Baby Dolls, Beatrice Hill led a revolt against another set of similarly placed women who were rivals because of their politics of turf and caste warfare. This revolt involved taking over one of the dances being sponsored by the rival group. Wearing sharp-looking clothes was part of the strategy. Beatrice recalled Sam Bonart wondering aloud why all those African Americans were coming in his store and buying up all the evening clothes. Sam avidly engaged in civic participation by serving as the president of the Young Men's Hebrew Association, as trustee of the Jewish Federation of Charities, treasurer of the Orthodox Congregation Beth Israel, and as a member of the Playground Commission. The latter contribution would bring him lasting recognition in New Orleans because he provided a space for play that Joseph Lee, founder of the playground movement, felt was critical for adults to rejuvenate themselves.[24]

THE "NEW WOMAN" AND THE OLD POVERTY

The vitality of such women as Beatrice Hill was constructed against a backdrop of severe race, gender, and class oppression, denying their recognition on a par with the Zulu Social Aid and Pleasure Club, the Black Indians of New Orleans, and the Skull and Bones Gang. Understanding the sociopolitical world of the Million Dollar Baby Dolls is key to understanding them as the courageous and trailblazing women that they were. Black Creole women who were born between 1885 and 1905 would have to contend, for their entire lives, with the consequences of racial repression and legal segregation. It would affect every aspect of their lives. Their restricted access to education, healthcare, and employment would determine their level of literacy and longevity as well as their ability to accumulate wealth. It was not unusual for Black girls to end their education in third grade in order to enter the workforce, formally or informally. Occupations open to Black women were limited to sewing, laundering, being a domestic servant in a White household, and to lesser degrees factory work and teaching. For example, according to Arthé Anthony, for the first quarter of the twentieth century White-owned and -operated cigar companies maintained "whites only" employment policies, or allowed unsatisfactory segregated working conditions for their African American employees.[25] The circumstances surrounding Black people's working conditions led Eugenia Lacarra, a Black Creole born at the turn of the century, to wonder: "I stop to think sometimes, and I wonder how the poor colored people got along. You couldn't work in the department stores, the men couldn't drive a bus, you couldn't work for the telephone company, you couldn't work for the Public Service, so if you didn't do menial labor, or housework, or learn to be a cigar maker, or you weren't lucky enough to get an education to teach, well, you were in very bad luck because then these people had nothing to do. You see, they didn't give the poor colored people jobs."[26]

The depth of this poverty becomes poignantly alive through childhood recollections of Danny Barker. As a child, Barker visited his father in the District. His father lived with a woman, Celie, who owned a boarding-house. The abysmal living conditions included a dump where defective and condemned imports were thrown away. The residents of Back o' Town would search among the goods for what was salvageable.[27]

Black women also were victimized by sexual abuse. This problem was pervasive in the South and was widely known but seldom discussed. Both Black men and women suffered sexual stigmatization, with women being defined as "sexually loose" while men were depicted as "rapists." This was the period in which Ida Wells led her "crusade for justice," exposing the practice of lynching Black people on false charges of sexual aggression. So widespread was the problem of Black women's sexual victimization that recent research by historian Danielle McGuire places it squarely in the center of the civil rights movement,[28] inciting the Montgomery Improvement Association's famous bus boycott.

White men's sexual aggression across the color line was felt by Black women in New Orleans. For example, as a teenager, Amelda Betz, a black New Orleanian, worked as a nanny for a white family with two small children: the Kanton family. Her parents, however, did not want her to work for the Kantons because, as Betz explained in an interview, "at that time my daddy and momma knew about Mr. Kanton's record."[29] When the interviewer asked what type of record, Betz replied, "Well, he used to love colored girls, you see. [His wife] didn't know, but all the colored people knew."[30]

The Million Dollar Baby Dolls were proud of their independence and made no excuses for their life choices. They created an art form by drawing on the tools of their culture, united in entrepreneurial sisterhood, and turned the street into their platform. Nevertheless, minimization of New Orleans Black women's expressive culture continues, both in mainstream society and in academia.[31] If this is true for the most visible and "respectable" of Black women such as business owner Gertrude Geddis Willis, singer Mahalia Jackson, and educators Henriette Delille, Alice Ruth Moore Dunbar-Nelson, and Frances Joseph-Gaudet, just to name a few, the invisibility of the creative entrepreneurship, collectivist activities, and contribution to the history of Mardi Gras of Beatrice Hill, Leola Tate, and Althea Brown is virtually guaranteed. If the drug and alcohol abuse of Black male jazz musicians is considered a normalized condition of their work and creative environment and the study of all aspects of their creativity is vigorously undertaken,[32] why is no such scholarly equity extended to women who engaged in a profession that was legal, even if scorned, and who took the nothing they were given and produced a legacy that was imitated by the "respectable" classes of Black women and men for decades to come?

AFRICAN AMERICAN DANCE

To be a woman who "danced the jazz" in the age of Jim Crow, as a Black woman in New Orleans, was to be part of a subversive underground. Jazz was considered outsider music, and the Million Dollar Baby Dolls were outsiders to middle-class Black "respectable"[33] culture and to all of White society. The Baby Dolls embraced their outsider identities and combined them with the freedoms being assumed by the New Woman of the 1920s. The period between 1890 and 1920 saw a revolution in social and political norms governing women in the United States. Women had agitated and subsequently were successful in winning the vote. They were making forays into formerly male-dominated spaces from the professions to the saloons. Dance became a major tool by which women of all social classes defined and expressed their changing relationship to their autonomy and sexuality.[34]

Early African American Dancing in New Orleans

African and Afro-Caribbean dancing took place in Congo Square. The dancers were reported to attach animal skins to their clothing, which may be evidence that they performed African masquerade dancing. They performed the *bamboula,* a serious dance involving bowing, curtseying, and eventually involving all body parts as the tempo of the drum increased. Onlookers, especially women, would sing a chorus, clap, and chant. Other dances included the Afro-Caribbean *calenda* and the *chica*. African influences on the dancers were without question. Barbara Glass has noted that "improvisatory call and response singing, dance moves signaled by the drum, circle and line formations, the presence of the community to support and encourage the dancers, percussion provided by both the drums and by handclapping, and movement expressive of sexuality or fertility" were always present.[35]

Jazz Age Dancing

The Jazz Age was about dancing, and dance music ensured sales of records and sheet music. Composers and lyricists found themselves under pressure from music publishers to make sure their music was danceable. There were two popular tempos: fast and slow. The fast-tempo music was accompanied by steps like the stomp that emerged from the New Orleans brass-band marching tradition. Its use most famously was for jazz funerals. Brass bands played dirges and hymns on the way to the cemetery. On the way back from the cemetery, when the body had been "cut loose," the mourners danced to up-tempo religious hymns and moved on to "hot," raucous music. In the dance halls, New Orleanians were performing dances with names like "the shag," "hop," "jump," "grind," "twist," "belly rub," "strut," "wiggle," "Ball and the Jack," the "Black Bottom" and many others that had no names. Mostly, these were called shake dances.

Nude Dancing

Two types of dances are of note for their popularity in the District's brothels, dance halls, and saloons. One is the "naked dance," and the other is the "ham-kick." In the early days of the striptease, women were undressed by others. In a nod to Victorian standards, the woman in the act was "innocent" in that she did not engage brazenly in displaying herself. Her nudity was caused by others.[36] The Million Dollar Baby Dolls would strip the clothes off one of the dancers, and she would be nude on stage. New Orleans native Tony Jackson, an accomplished composer and pianist, wrote a tune, "The Naked Dance," that was played when women of the District disrobed. The ham-kick was a form of competition in which a proprietor would hang a ham from a rafter and women who wore no underwear would kick at it in a mock attempt to knock it down. The woman who kicked the highest won the ham. The Million Dollar Baby Dolls were known for their high kicks.

Second-line Dancing

Danny Barker credits Bou-Boul Fortune (pronounced *For-tu-nay*), a rival of jazz legend Buddy Bolden, as the first bandleader to label the band as the "first line" and the band's supporters as the "second line." The second line consists of community members who dance to the music the band plays as it marches or has a procession or parade down neighborhood streets. Frederic Ramsey described the relationship between dance and the Black brass band as being centrally focused on dance from its inception.

> From the beginning, the music of Negro Brass bands both in New Orleans and Alabama seems to have been related to dancing. This alone would not distinguish them from the earliest white bands known in Alabama or elsewhere; but it is unlikely that white audiences indulged in the sort of loose-hipped dancing which accompanies both the New Orleans or Alabama bands' music. One can see the sort of dancing flowing along in the Second Line that follows a funeral band in New Orleans today. . . . In New Orleans, the bands have played traditionally, for festive occasions, and for funerals. . . . The rhythm set up by these bands is not a tight, regular march step; it is more of a flowing, anticipatory emphasis and counteremphasis, ideally suited to [an improvised] style of dance.[37]

The second line and its music are sometimes interpreted as an expression of resistance to oppression when poor people take over public streets in processions. The second line is also valued for the spiritual communion it engenders among family and friends. In 1959, Marshall and Jean Stearns witnessed a second-line parade in the heart of the city and described how the dance conveyed the spirit of the music: "It was not just the music—we heard the same or better on recordings—the dancing, a fascinating variety of walks, shuffles, grinds, struts, prances, and kicks, improvised, by the marchers—official and unofficial—as the residents rushed out of their houses to join the parade. The dancing gave the music a new dimension of joy and vitality."[38]

Shot of the characters of the Baby Dolls from *Fat Tuesday (and All That Jazz)!,* a ballet that featured the Arthur Hall Dance Company and was conceived, produced, and directed by Wesley O. Brustad. A number of Arthur Hall Dance Company members performed the role of the Baby Dolls, including Delphine Mantz, Ruth Mills, Sharon Ingram, Andrea Vinson, and Regina Taitts. Photograph reproduced courtesy Wesley O. Brustad.

Putting It All Together

Fat Tuesday and All That Jazz is a jazz ballet commemorating the African American–inspired New Orleans Mardi Gras and its dance, music, and costuming pageantry. Choreographed by the Arthur Hall Afro-American Dance Ensemble and featuring Dejan's Olympia Brass Band, the ballet has been performed on stage and broadcast on PBS. It features West African and African American dances. Notably, the Baby Dolls have a central role in the ballet. Writing of the performance delivered by the Chicago Muntu Dance Theatre, Sid Smith noted that "there are traditional African moves in the form of an opening processional, but, before the finale, a wide range of American pop dances from the 20th Century get their salute. . . . Hall's work is a modern ballet dressed in the moves of jazz and the Caribbean, buoyed by the music of Dixieland jazz, rhythm and blues and folk." *Fat Tuesday* chronicles a classic melodramatic story of young lovers Kid Bunky and Mimi Pechet; a villainous card shark; and a seductive woman, Mamie Desdoumes. Smith described the Baby Dolls' performance as being "a saucy tap trio."[39]

Couples dancing at a Baby Doll celebration, 1942, Mardi Gras in New Orleans. From the Collection of the U.S. Works Progress Administration of Louisiana, courtesy State Library of Louisiana.

Couple dancing at a Baby Doll celebration, at San Jacinto Club and Dance Hall, 1422 Dumaine Street, New Orleans. From the Collection of the U.S. Works Progress Administration of Louisiana, courtesy State Library of Louisiana.

Couple dancing at the Baby Doll celebration. From the Collection of the
U.S. Works Progress Administration
of Louisiana, courtesy State Library of
Louisiana.

BABY DOLLS AND DANCE

Some of the original Baby Dolls made their living in the brothels and dance
halls, innovating on dance steps popular in their day. Robert McKinney
captures the spirit of working-class social dance parties in his description
of Saturday "front parlor" "Shakedown Dances" where dancers dressed in
"any kind of clothes desired from overalls to shimmies." Food was served,
generally consisting of whiskey and sandwiches. A pianist and drummer
provided live music. These were free parties where "lights are always dark,
dancing close and the guest drunk."[40]

The families in the Tremé used their homes as hubs of entertainment for their large families, and the arts were central to their gatherings. Families, friends, and neighbors danced to popular tunes, to "hot"
music, and to Creole songs. On Carnival Day, some of these families took
their singing, dancing, and costuming as Baby Dolls and hit the streets.
Lyle Saxon relates a story illustrating the symbiotic relationship between
the drummer and dancer that has been embedded in Black New Orleans
culture from the days of Congo Square. Saxon tells of a young White boy
who was entrusted to an African American family servant on Carnival Day.

The servant, Robert, put the boy in a mask so they could pass undetected as to their race and go into Black clubs and other Black-dominated spaces with little notice. Saxon portrays Robert as intent on partying all Mardi Gras Day. He was not going to let his little charge get in the way of a good time. Robert knew all the top Black haunts and located the dance hall and saloon where King Zulu was holding court, the High Brown Social and Athletic Club. Sitting on King Zulu's lap was a woman wearing a short red dress. There is no evidence to suggest that she was a Baby Doll per se, but her short-skirted personage drinking with King Zulu signifies the ambition and desire not uncommon for men and women rebelling against the social restrictions of the 1920s Jim Crow South.

Saxon describes a women's dance contest. What is of significance is not that the women were competing against each other for the prize of King Zulu's attention but the style of their dance and the rapt attention and enthusiasm they generated in the crowd, including the musicians:

> And the members of the orchestra laid aside their instruments and turned about in their chairs in order to watch. All except the drummer. His big drum was moved further out upon the dancing floor and he began beating out a measured rhythm.
>
> To the center of the floor came a woman, a thin quadroon. She began to shake in time with the drumbeats, first a shoulder, then a hip. Then she began to squirm and lunge. At each beat of the drum her position would change, and as the measured beating continued she moved her body with each beat. At last she was shaking all over, head wagging, hips bobbing back and forth. And as the drumbeats became more rapid, her gyrations became more violent. At the end of a few minutes the drumming stopped and she stood limp in the center of the floor.
>
> There was wild applause.
>
> She retired and another girl took her place, this time a black girl. Her movements were more suggestive, more animalish—and pleased the crowd more extravagantly than the first dancer had done. The drumming was done in the same fashion as at first. When she had finished a third girl took her place.[41]

The winner of the contest, was, according to Saxon, "a large, fat, black girl, dressed in a yellow dress. Her face shone with grease and sweat, but she was proud and happy with her success."[42]

Even as late as the 1940s and 1950s, the Baby Dolls' jazz entrepreneurship endured. Anita Thomas, the aunt of Sylvester Francis, founder of the Backstreet Cultural Museum in the Tremé, was a member of and gave dances with the Satin Sinners Baby Dolls group and was a Big Queen of the Eighth Ward Hunters Black Indian Gang. It was Mr. Francis's emphatic narration of his aunt's significance in Black Carnival that helped me to realize the significance of the Baby Dolls in their community.

Similarly, Andrew Justin, a native New Orleanian born in 1942, learned to sew from his mother Anna and his grandmother Geneva Lopice, who owned the Carr-Lopice Funeral Home located in the Tremé. Influenced by the neighborhood's Indians, he grew up to form his own tribe called the Wild Tremé. "Anna and her sister Pauline Guillemet were Baby Dolls. A sisterhood of promiscuous maskers who cavorted on Fat Tuesday in the first half of the twentieth century, Baby Dolls wore skimpy pink outfits— short skirts, bloomers, satin blouses, and bonnets tied under their chins with ribbons." They were, recalls Chief Drew, a rough-and-tumble bunch: "Kick a man in his ass."[43] These women challenged traditional notions of feminine domesticity because their environment was tough. Wages were low for Black people, and women in Andrew's family relied on the informal economy. Anna was the mother of nine children, including twins who died. Anna and her female relatives gave fish fries and waistline parties, in which the cost of admission was based on the width of one's abdomen. She made pralines for sale, took in laundry for Whites, and worked for decades at a factory making belts. When money was tight, she and the other women met the sailors at the ports and earned enough to feed the family. This work in the informal economy allowed the women in Chief Drew's family to give food to the poor people in Tremé, to care for their own children, and to buy the materials necessary to mask as Baby Dolls on Carnival.

On Carnival they all came out together, dressed, recalls Chief Drew, in fine silk and linen. They wore socks or tights with two-inch heel shoes. They wore bloomers with ruffles and lace. They would also sport razors and ice picks, if someone dared to touch them. They would sing songs like "I'll Fly Away" as they paraded, and the Baby Dolls had a kazoo band accompanying them.[44]

Arthé Anderson observes that Black Creoles born at the turn of the century were not as likely to migrate west and north as other Black New Orleanians. Black Creoles had access to the building trades, which provided them with enough money to purchase their homes and to sustain the rich cultural life they had inherited from previous generations. Joseph Lee, the inventor of the playground movement, believed that, when adults engaged in play, they were renewing their lives. He came to the conclusion that White culture could learn from the tendency in Black culture to "never lose hope for the future nor a sense of joy of living."[45] In spite of the suffocating discrimination, Black New Orleanians had managed to build play into their lives. Every family had a musician, singer, or dancer who could easily become a local celebrity. Saints' days and holy days were frequent and required family preparation. The culture was given to humor and light-heartedness, as can be seen in the practice of giving pet names to children that lasted throughout their lifetimes.[46] And the whole community had Carnival, or as the locals called it, "Old Fools Day," during which you could "be anything you want to be." There was a vitality that was built into everyday Black life.

The Million Dollar Baby Dolls danced and organized and innovated on the vital elements in Black New Orleans culture. Living in the Progressive Era, they were part of the wave that women dancers like Irene Castle were riding by tapping into their own desires to shed Victorian restraints on their ability to earn income as women, to dress in less restricted fashions, to experience their sexuality, and to be a force in their world. On a national level, Castle was creating a place for the independent sexual woman; in New Orleans parlance, "she masked." According to Lewis Erenberg, Irene "remained a girl; she never achieved an image of a mature woman." She fostered an image of the dancing woman as an "elegant American girl." "Even to dabble with what little female sensuality was expressed in the dance required that women become girls, safely isolated from the dangerous knowledge they were beginning to acquire."[47] Women like Castle opened a space for middle- and upper-class White women to participate in sensual social dancing by constructing the image of the adult female as "both sexual and innocent." The Million Dollar Baby Dolls would turn this concept on its head. They combined short skirts, soft pastel colors, and blonde curly wigs with sensual dance on the streets and an attitude that gave little care to what others thought. They surely must have sent fear up the spines of men who were part of a generation beginning to lose control over women.

It would be little wonder that this generation would experience an unprec-edented number of wildly popular songs about women as babies and dolls. Expressing both the excitement and titillation of grown-up women acting coy and innocent as a girl and paradoxically wishing that the New Woman was more childlike, songs burst on the scene to define the changing ar-rangements between the sexes.

3

"Oh You Beautiful Doll"

The Baby Doll as a National Sex Symbol in the Progressive Era

SONGS CELEBRATING women as "dolls" and "babies" flourished in the early years of the twentieth century. "Oh, You Beautiful Doll," written by A. Seymour Brown (1911), and "Pretty Baby," created by musician and New Orleans native Tony Jackson (1912 or earlier), and other similarly titled numbers were part of the new and popular ragtime music. "When the Grown Up Ladies Act like Babies (I've Got to Love 'Em That's All)" (1914), by Maurice Abrahams, Joe Young, and Edgar Leslie, is a further indication of what was titillating male desire at the time. The actress Florence Mills wore a baby doll costume and performed with composer Tony Jackson as a "Pretty Baby" with her Panama Trio around 1918. On the flip side, Bessie Smith's "Baby Doll" (1926) expressed women's desire to be someone special to a special someone: "I want to be somebody's baby doll so I can get my loving all the time. I want to be somebody's baby doll to ease my mind." "Baby Dollism" was in the air. It was a part of the national sensual ethos. In New Orleans, one clever group of African American women seized on the emerging icon and turned it into a marketing strategy and an expressive art.

Jackson's "Pretty Baby" rag was specially written to accompany erotic dancing that characterized entertainment in the District after midnight. His lyrics described how a person in love with an adult is just like a person loving a baby:

Tony Jackson accompanying the Panama Trio, formed by Florence Mills with Carolyn Williams and Cora Green, about 1918. Photograph by Duncan P. Schiedt, used with permission.

Won't you come and let me rock you in my cradle of love
And we'll cuddle all the time.
Oh, I want a lovin' baby, and it might as well be you,
Pretty baby of mine.

It is thought that Jackson wrote this for his male lover and the words were more explicit in the original. Another jazz musician, Clarence Williams, who was well acquainted with the sporting scene of Black New Orleans, wrote the popular "You're Some Pretty Doll" (1917). His lyrics go to the heart of male fantasy of sexual play:

> Now listen Dolly, come over here
> There's something I must whisper in your ear
> You've got me hanging 'round you like a child
> It seems as if you're goin' to drive me wild.

Williams's song captures many of the features of the Million Dollar Baby Dolls. The "Doll" not only makes him nervous, i.e., "sets my heart jumping," but will make him "fall."

> Those charming little curls and dimples too
> They make me know that it is you, just you
> I wonder if your dear heart is mine
> If so, it is a joy divine,
> Oh! won't you tell me and put my heart at ease
> Oh! for a loving squeeze.[1]

The song ends with a declaration that he has "millions" that he will spend on his pretty doll.

In his "Fragment of an Autobiography," Ferdinand "Jelly Roll Morton" LaMothe recalled that, in the District, prostitutes stood "in their cribs with their chippies on." He noted that a chippie was a dress that "women wore, knee length, very easy to disrobe."[2] Morton's signature sentence, "The chippies in their little-girl dresses were standing in the crib doors singing the blues," captured the fantasy that some men were willing to pay for and a group of women used as one economic option under the restricted employment opportunities available to them. Historian Samuel Kinser views the Baby Doll tradition as being borrowed from a similar practice in Trinidad. While the direct line cannot be proven, and the available evidence does not support this assertion, he rightly concludes that male libido was aroused by the image.

"MIND YUH BABY": BABY DOLLS AND TRINIDAD'S CARNIVAL

From the inception of their participation in Carnival, Afro-Caribbeans would critique their conditions of bondage and oppression. As newly freed Africans in the Caribbean began to participate in Trinidad's Carnival around 1832, the colonial authorities as well as the White and Black elite were alarmed and scandalized. The revelers dramatized characters from folklore or historic persons, and some were novel expressions of European Carnival personalities.[3] Over time, they invented numerous Carnival characters and masks that satirized the practices of the ruling class. One satirical *mas* was the Baby Doll, which Dylan Kerrigan describes in the following way:

> In her short, frilly dress, exposing her legs, and her large poke bonnet or mob-cap, the baby doll—named for her eponymous accessory, a child's doll—was already a common sight during Carnival in the 1860s and 1870s, the period of *Jamette* Carnival. Sometimes she roamed alone, sometimes in pairs or groups, but the masquerade was always the same: the baby doll pursued any respectable gentleman she encountered on the street with piercing cries of "Mister! Mister! Look your child!" embarrassing him into forking over money for support of the hypothetical infant.
>
> This clever routine spoke to one of the realities of life under slavery and in its aftermath, when many slave-owners fathered children with their servants, only to refuse to recognize these illegitimate offspring.
>
> One of the paradoxes of the baby doll was that she herself usually dressed like the infant whose mother she was meant to portray—in a simple child's dress. Originally she wore a full wire mask, later reduced to a half-mask covering just her eyes, and finally no mask at all.[4]

Philip Scher wrote that old-time Trinidad carnival costuming traditions were accompanied by scripted speeches. Samantha Noel argues that Carnival offered Afro-Caribbean Baby Doll maskers the opportunity to speak their minds.[5] The maskers would accuse both Black and White men of neglecting and abandoning their responsibilities to their children. In addition, in dressing as a baby, the adult herself or himself was a living symbol of the pathos of feeling neglected by the family and the state. Noel's analysis springs from the drawing "Carnival on Frederick Street, Port of Spain," published May 5, 1888, by Melton Prior, an English illustrator and war correspondent whose drawings appeared in the *Illustrated London News.* Noel speculates that underlying the priest's stoic expression is shock and annoyance. His emotional reaction stemmed from being close to a woman he would consider his social inferior. His upset was at being singled out by her for condemnation.

Whether it was a dark-skinned woman carrying a blue-eyed baby doll or two men playing the *mas* (one dressed as a Baby Doll and the other a policeman who would get the accused to give some money to the Baby Doll), Kerrigan notes, "in the early decades of the 20th century, baby doll *mas* became less and less frequent on the streets of Port of Spain, but never entirely disappeared. Today she is most likely to be found at *J'Ouvert* or at special theatrical presentations of traditional *mas* characters, still reminding onlookers with her haunting, taunting cry of a painful phenomenon in Trinidad's social history."

Just as the New Orleans Baby Dolls emerged from the cultural mix of immediate environment, so also did the Baby Dolls of Trinidad according to anthropologist John Cupid. Cupid suggested that "the Trinidad baby doll has a distinct origin. She is a woman looking for her husband, the child's father. . . . The sailors and soldiers who came from the Second World War weren't the start of this character. Instead they carried on a reality dating back to the slave period, when slave masters separated children from their fathers. With emancipation, the baby doll character evolved as an ironic release from the torturous conditions of their recent past."[6]

It is important to note the distinction between the Baby Doll practices in Trinidad and in New Orleans. In New Orleans, Baby Dolls are in no way asking for money for their children. The shaming of men because of their neglect of children is solely a Trinidad custom. Baby Dolls in New Orleans traditionally either engaged in showy displays of their own money, tucking it in their garters and bloomers, or in some instances, those who were prostitutes might, if so inclined, turn tricks during their processions. Hence Harnett Kane's euphemistic description of Baby Dolls as "dark girls of more than goodwill." From its inception, the New Orleans tradition had nothing to do with women's domesticity and maternalism but was all about the woman herself, as beautiful, sexy, powerful, dominant, proud, and tough.

"MIGHTY PROUD": WOMEN RETURN TO THE STREETS
ON MARDI GRAS IN NEW ORLEANS

In the waning days of the nineteenth century, the women of New Orleans began returning to the streets as masked participants after having been ousted through the emergence of organized parades by upper-class White men who formed krewes in the mid-1850s. The original Creole practice of Carnival, which was inclusive, random, and informal, had changed so that class and race came to define who could participate in the public square. Women who masked became stigmatized, and the association between masking on Carnival in public and being a prostitute would be the ruling view until women re-appropriated the streets by acting out a stigmatized identity and by forming their own krewes.

One of the earliest women's krewes, Les Mysterieuses (1896–1900), was formed by an upper-class group. While they did not parade, they held a ball and reversed the gender roles. Male krewes had been giving balls and requiring women to come in evening attire while the men would mask and behave in ways that suited themselves. Les Mysterieuses required women to mask at their ball but did not allow men to enter if they were in costume. Subsequent groups were the Mittens (1901), Les Inconnues (1901), the Mystic Maids (1906), the Krewe of Yami (1911), the Krewe of Iris (1922), and the Krewe of Les Marionettes (1922). Several Black women's krewes were formed as well: the Red Circle, Young Ladies 23, and the Mystic Krewe. None of these all-women's groups paraded.[7] In 1941, the Krewe of Venus interrupted the all-male street parades to officially roll with a dozen floats. Venus came to be expected at mid-afternoon the Sunday before Mardi Gras. In 1959, the Krewe of Iris began to parade. Like Venus, they paraded in the afternoon, but days before Mardi Gras, an even less prestigious position.[8] In recent times, the women's Mardi Gras clubs and parades follow the masculine tradition. Writing about the Krewe of Muses, the first women's night-parading group, organized in 2000, Robin Roberts notes their appropriation of aspects of male privilege during Mardi Gras festivities. These aspects are masking, producing a *tableau*,[9] selecting a court, choosing dance partners, and especially parading after dark. Nevertheless, Muses seized opportunities during their elaborate festival preparations to mock gender norms and playfully and humorously use emblems that were stereotypically feminine.[10]

A sense of what it meant to Black women to ride on the floats and in limousines as the object of longing, admiration, envy, or amusement comes from the oral histories of women who were queens of "Zulu and the Amazons" in the late 1930s. Catherine Riley may well have been one of the first female queens of Zulu and the Amazons. The tall, brown-skinned, I.C. Beer Parlor waitress lived and worked in the heart of the Black commercial district as well as at the center of New Orleans's Black cultural economy, South Rampart Street. Catherine learned the protocol and manners of being a queen from Josephine Smith, who had served in that capacity for two years. According to Catherine, Josephine was more "society-like" than she was. In fact, Catherine was comfortable with the residents of a "lowly tenement" house on Julia Street. Robert McKinney reported, "Aware of the reflection on her character caused by residence in this particular house— for her neighbors are notoriously fast in their living as a race horse in the stretch, she yet flatly denied the implication emphasizing the difference with the statement, 'I don't go for that kind of stuff. I work for mine.'"

The cost associated with being a king or a queen in the Zulu parade was quite hefty. Catherine noted that irony when she said that, rather than others giving parties for her, she was expected to host revelers. She was specially selected by John Metoyer, a founder of the Zulu Social and Pleasure Club who apparently was smitten by her during the Carnival season of 1937 and sought her coronation the next year. The negatives for Catherine included the gossip, the people rushing her and pulling on her clothes during the parade, the reporters wanting to get a story from her, as well as the expense and the subsequent hounding by debt collectors. Yet she confessed that being queen made her "mighty proud" when her friends saw her riding on the float. It made her proud too that she could throw trinkets to parade-goers. "I enjoyed all of that."[11]

At age twenty-five, Odette Delille was the 1939 queen of Zulu and the Amazons. She was from a close-knit Catholic Creole family where it was understood that each family member had to take care of him- or herself. Odette attended Craig School but had to drop out when her mother became ill. After a three-week illness, her mother died. Odette had three sisters, two of whom worked at nightclubs. Hilda worked at the Elite (a favorite haunt of the Million Dollar Baby Dolls), and Stella worked at the Snow Flake. They had a brother, Leon, who worked at Harlem Grill. An exceptionally hard worker, Odette was employed at Haspel's, the men's suit-making company, as a factory worker. Due to new federal labor laws, Haspel's increased the workers' wages, provided vacation time, and took out funds for Social Security. In spite of the raise, the changes in the laws reduced Odette's take-home pay, forcing her to seek additional employment. She had been waitressing at Dileo's beer parlor on Ursuline and Robertson three nights a week for about eight months when Zulu members Leopold LeBlanc and John Metoyer asked her if she would like to be queen. Apparently Dileo was willing to contribute a large sum to the organization, and that was the motivation for the decision. According to Odette, patronage increased substantially when the announcement was made that the queen of Zulu and the Amazons worked at Dileo's.

Odette could hardly believe her good fortune. She had never masked before, nor even gone outside her neighborhood, and now she would see parts of Carnival that she hadn't imagined. She would have four maids as part of her court, all wearing sky-blue velvet dresses, gold capes, gold slippers, gold crowns, and pink roses with gold ribbons. The court was supplying Odette her crown and mantle; her sister was giving her calla lilies. On Carnival Day she would toast the king at Geddes and Moss Funeral Home, have pictures taken with him, and then would join him, not on a float but in a car with her maids. They paraded through the city and down to Gallier Hall[12] to toast the mayor. The parade would meander and stop at every merchant who contributed money. While she knew that the court was supposed to drink at every spot, unlike Catherine Riley who described herself as "so high it wasn't even funny," Odette was planning to abstain. "If I have a drink at every stop by the time Carnival is over, I won't know myself. I don't want to fool with none of the liquor. I really can have a good time without drinking."

After the parade, she would attend the Zulu after-party. Eight days later, there would be a cake-cutting event. Odette would wear a white velvet and chiffon gown with silver slippers and receive presents from her boyfriend, her relatives, and her father, along with the adulation of her community. As for the opportunity to be the queen, Odette was notified in person: "they just sent the officials to tell me" and "I felt proud."[13]

Ceola Carter had an unlikely path to the crown in 1940. She migrated from Morgan City, where Blacks had been engaged in jobs integral to coastal communities and domestic work since before slavery. In 1917, when Ceola was about two years old, Hollywood made the first Tarzan film in Morgan City due to its jungle-like appearance. Ceola seems to have been targeted by older men in the community who preyed on young girls. She had been sexualized early, and this seems to have been known in the community. Nonetheless, Ceola's spirit refused to be crushed, and she aspired for more. She probably left Morgan City after her mother passed. She had fifty dollars from her minister, free whiskey and money from older men, and insurance money received after her mother's death. When she left, at about eighteen, people advised her not to worry. Her community predicted that, since she was "born under the sign of Saturn," honor would always come her way.

But her first day in New Orleans was most inauspicious. It found her in a fight with a man, in jail, and in front of a judge who issued a strong admonition for her to go back home, which she seriously considered. Ceola worked as a domestic, a waitress, and lived with boyfriends who often met unfortunate ends such as incarceration or even death. But her spirit was indefatigable, as was her luck with getting their money when they disappeared from the scene. At age twenty-seven, Ceola Carter had a good man, a "good" job, and was queen of Zulu and the Amazons. She ruled from the Geddes and Moss limousine; she wore white satin and lace, a multicolored train with a collar of green marabou, long white gloves, a rhinestone crown, and carried a white bag, all gifts from her former employer for whom she had worked as a maid. She asserted that "I'm doing what I think any woman might do under the circumstances—having my fun. How I have it is my business; the Queen's Business!"[14]

CARNIVAL'S UNRULY WOMEN

Women's visibility in Carnival is more appropriately located as a terrain of struggle; it is a field of competing and contradictory desires where acts of libidinal self-assertion exist uneasily with the pleasures and real dangers of commodification and fetishism.
—Natasha Barnes

Since as early as the fifteenth century, Carnival has been associated with dancing, parading in the streets in masks, visiting neighbors and establishments, and with sexual freedom and sexual display. Women's bodily expression during Carnival qualifies as performance. That is to say that women's visibility, via their revealing costumes, dancing, singing, and parading on public streets in front of a viewing audience, is often intended to make certain kinds of statements. According to Belinda Edmondson,[15] when women allowed themselves to be viewed publicly, political commentary was plentiful and often followed by state and social attempts at regulating their behavior. As Sarah Carpenter wryly observed, "The faults here attributed to masking are precisely those traditionally held against the unruly descendants of Eve: curiosity, garrulousness, envy and scandal."[16]

Historically, carnival revelry and masked identities offered an opportunity for women's sexual desire to be experienced in novel ways without the burdens of accountability. Female costumes that were considered revealing in their time were often accompanied by performances of songs, often bawdy, and dances, often suggestive. These were considered troubling behaviors for the established social order. Ken Plummer suggests that, for sexual behavior to be seen as a problem for society, a group of people has to organize it as such and articulate reasons for objection. They have to be convinced that the behavior is "wrong." The behavior must be practiced by a sizable number of people. The opposing group must also believe that the offensive behavior is amenable to being changed. The opposing group becomes determined to do something about it.[17]

Once targeted, the behavior rises to the level of sexual spectacle because it challenges the morals, values, and hierarchies of the prevailing social order. Women's carnival masking elicits social anxieties relating to desire, disease, and traditional heterosexual monogamous behavior. Reactions to women's masking can be considered an example of moral panic because the festive activities are interpreted as a challenge, a confrontation, and an inversion of the dominant and dominating value system. These public attacks are pursued with vigor because, in Plummer's view, "sexuality appears to be a major device used to tap into all sorts of social anxieties, to generate panic, and to demarcate boundaries. Studies point to many different sources of these anxieties and boundary mapping, but they include anxieties over gender roles, heterosexuality and the family; the importance of reproduction and pronatalism; concerns over the role of youth and childhood; race and racialized categories; the divisions between classes and 'class fears' just to name a few."[18]

The motives behind the Baby Doll masking tradition are varied. Pamela Franco reminds us that the cultures of Africa used masquerade in very specific ways: to portray ancestors as mentors and educators for initiation ceremonies, and as mediators between the spirit world and the human one. Enslavement and colonial rule changed Africans' ability to reconstruct their practices in the New World. As a result, they appropriated the European Carnival celebrations to address their concerns with representation (which was derogatory) and to reposition themselves, at least symbolically.[19] One group of women maskers, the Caribbean *jamet,* illustrates this well. Edmondson describes the *jamet*—a word with possible French origins connected to *diameter,* or to be below the diameter of respectable society—as serving as a thorn in the side of the colonial authorities: "The term 'jamette' refers to black women in nineteenth-century urban Trinidad, black women who were associated with the barracks yards, gangs, and the streets. (Originally the term refers to female stick fighters; stick fighting is considered a male sport.) These disreputable women . . . were also active as 'chanterelles,' or calypso singers, and their 'carisos' songs, were habitually castigated as being lewd and erotic, and for allegedly instigating obscene dancing."[20] Franco characterizes the *jamet* as issuing social criticism through the *mas* and interprets the *mas* as portraying the "unruly woman" whose "performance style is usually loud, boisterous, inflammatory and, sometimes, erotic."[21]

Franco interrogated two types of practices: the *pissenlit* and the stick-fighter. The *pissenlit* (or "bedwetter"; these women wore a nightgown and displayed a replica of a soiled menstrual cloth) was particularly provocative. Franco notes that *jamet* women were considered prostitutes. Whether they were or not, conviction rates for the rape of Black women were abysmal; beyond that, women could be locked up by unscrupulous policemen if they did not submit sexually. Once confronted with the courts, women would have to undergo invasive exams. The *pissenlit,* Franco asserts, signaled to the authorities that they had "blood on their hands." In response to the challenge by the women's sexual spectacles, the state mobilized. In 1895, the *pissenlit* costume was banned. Cross-dressing women who engaged in street fighting with other women continued to be worrisome. Franco concluded that the *pissenlit* "embarrassed the state through a reversal of its condemnation of her. The stickfighting woman inverted the Victorian aesthetic of femininity. . . . The response to these two Carnival characters was severe—fines, incarceration and possible deportation—primarily because the women's performances were 'socially unbounded.' Despite the harsh responses, *jamet* women continued to exhibit independence."[22]

Samantha Noel also theorized that the colonial response was to reinforce British values and dicta. Women, according to the authorities, should observe propriety, modesty, maternalism, and fidelity to their husbands. Theirs was to be a muted and invisible presence. One way *jamets* defied these values was in their dance. They "boasted their skill and bravery, verbal wit, talent in song, dance, and drumming, their indifference to the law, their sexual prowess, their familiarity with jail, and sometimes their contempt for the church. The women more often than not were the *chantuelles,* who sang praises of male stickfighters and used impromptu lyrics meant to shock and entertain; they wore masks and sometimes exposed their breasts."[23] "*Wining,*" Noel points out, "is an undulating and writhing form of dance that is concentrated in the pelvic area."[24] Noel links the history of modern-day wining currently performed at Carnival in Trinidad with its historic variations, including as practiced in Haiti and ultimately Africa, by citing Katherine Dunham's research on "the isolation of the hips in the *danses grouilles.*" Colonial authorities considered these movements vulgar and the lower classes who performed them as "the vulgate," or common people.

While many women masked, not all or even the majority fell into the *jamet* class. Edmondson divides female masking into the political categories of "the vulgar spectacle" and "the decorous spectacle." The vulgar she defines as transgressive, whereas "the socially approved, 'decorous'" spectacle is one that does the work of social uplift."[25] Franco explored the phenomenon of "dressing up" on Trinidad's Carnival whereby groups of women related by occupation or social interests wore the same attire. "Dressing up" and walking in a procession is the earliest form of being a "spectacular performer."[26] In the hands of Afro-Caribbean women, dressing up allowed them to connect to other historical periods in different countries. It also provided the imaginative play space to momentarily create alternative realities, along with opportunities to reclaim personal constructions of the self. Franco concluded that dressing up is a non-confrontational type of performance "that allows Afro-Creole women to be visible, not as objects, but as agents and producers of meaning in their Carnival performances."[27] Noel agrees with this line of thinking. For her, women now and in the past were able to use Carnival as a "lower frequency politics" which was not charged with generating political change per se, but was charged with maintaining "visible representation" for the overlooked and undervalued.

"THE BABIES AND THE DOLLS DON'T GIVE A DAMN"

The women and men who masked as Baby Dolls in the early days of the practice lived within the context of racism, classism, heteronormativity, and masculine privilege. But that hegemonic power met a cultural force of resistance. The Baby Dolls were pushed so far out of the mainstream that they ceased looking to White or middle-class norms for their sense of validation and virtue. They took the dominant cultural icons of the times and rearranged them to suit their own needs and purposes. By 1912, the image of the woman as Baby Doll had become a staple in music and movies. Slang terms for kin such as "momma," "poppa," and "baby" were being reappropriated into nicknames used in adult romantic relationships. In addition, the evolving children's culture introduced more toys, including baby dolls, for offspring of the middle and upper classes, creating a longing and sense of lack in poor girls everywhere.

Literary critic Trinna Frever defines the "doll" as a site for contested gender representation. Her study of feminist fiction in which dolls figure as a main trope reveals that their alternative perspective is an intervention and a confrontation with the forces of imperialism: racial, sexual, cultural, and economic. She sees three elements in conflict: the actual doll as cultural object, the woman-as-doll icon, and the real woman as a speaking, thinking, and acting subject. The doll as cultural icon and stereotypical figure places the control of women's representation in the hands of others, primarily men, who were the cultural and business brokers throughout the twentieth century.

Frever makes a number of assertions that apply to the manner in which the Million Dollar Baby Dolls reconfigured the images of the baby and the doll to transgress oppressive boundaries. Frever sees the women writers who take on the doll icon as reworking the "social messages of 'dollness'— and by association, girlhood, and womanhood—that circulate constantly through the popular culture in which they also participate."[28] The women writers create characters that break, burn, reframe, and reclaim the doll icon, affording "the survival of the girl and the woman, as represented in doll, as represented in fiction."[29] In demolishing the doll as cultural artifact, the woman writer "attempts to recreate herself in an image that is un-iconic: her own. This breaking open of the doll likewise opens the door for a range of subsequent literary and cultural depictions of identity and womanhood: complex, powerful, shifting, ambiguous, and beautiful."[30] This is what the Million Dollar Baby Dolls aspired to in their street performances.

THE BABY DOLL COSTUME

The most basic explanation of how the Baby Doll costume came into existence is the simple "at hand" nature of the clothes women wore in the

SALE

0010011468638082135

Description	SKU #	Amount
HE BABY DOLLS	005096	22.95

U B T O T A L		22.95
ales Tax 9.000%		2.07
O T A L S A L E		25.02
MasterCard/Visa	25.02	
O T A L T E N D E R		25.02

/13/2013 3:19:17 PM 001-082135

ssoc: MARGIT

redit Card Information:
Card Type : MasterCard/Visa
Card Nbr   : XXXXXXXXXXXX9858
Cardholder : BRIAN A SHEPLER

SALE

0010014ABBAB3098735

Description	SKU #	Amount
THE BABY DOLLS: UBCOGB		22.98

S U B T O T A L	22.98
Sales Tax 9.000%	2.07
T O T A L S A L E	25.02
MasterCard/Visa	25.02
T O T A L T E N D E R	25.02

7/13/2013 3:19:17 PM 001 082735
Assoc: MARGIT

Credit Card Information:
Card Type : MasterCard/Visa
Card Nbr   : XXXXXXXXXXXX8065
Cardholder : PRIJAH A SHEELER

Returns and exchanges must be made
within 30 days of purchase with the
original receipt present.

District as part of their trade. The "chippie" famously commemorated by Jelly Roll Morton[31] was a dress-like garment that stopped at about the knee and could be easily shed. And of course the tiny rooms used to ply the sex trade were called "cribs." When he was young and naive, jazz musician Sidney Bechet[32] was astonished to see women so briefly attired:

> I didn't know what all those women were doing hanging around the doorways in front of those houses. I'd go through and see them all there, standing around the way they do, waiting. They was all wearing those real short skirts and I saw them about, and it's the first time I recall any wondering about women like that. I was going through there and I looked at all those women and I asked my mother, "What are all those little girls doing standing like that?" I was just wondering about those skirts. They didn't look like little girls really, but I hadn't ever seen no women wearing clothes like that so I just up and asked my mother.[33]

Gerilyn G. Tandberg surveyed the clothing worn by women in the sex industry and identified the "Mother Hubbard" pajama as well as the chippie as two outer garments that allowed for easy access; these were clothes of convenience. In time, "chippie" had become slang for a woman of "easy virtue," and the outfit became associated with women prostitutes. Tandberg writes that "chippies mimicked the dress lengths of children, thus providing a link between the child's short skirts of the late 19th century and the fashionably accepted adult short skirt of the 1920s."[34] Up to that time, only a few groups of females could bare their limbs by wearing short skirts. The first, obviously, was little girls, and the other was women in the theater.

As women unafraid to break from the norm and live on the edge, women who worked as prostitutes were the first to adopt new fashion trends. It was to them that upper- and middle-class women looked to glean more liberating and stylish attire. Tandberg was taken aback to learn the degree to which sex workers were catalysts for effecting change in the aesthetics and tastes of the "respectable" class of women. Because women in the sex-work industry depended on their style and self-presentation to garner clients, they did not hesitate to breech social custom and wear styles that were innovative and daring. They gained the envy of respectable women who wanted to safeguard their reputations but who also wanted to express this free sense of style. Non-public women found ways to incorporate the keen fashion sense of the courtesan class.

Tandberg's synthesis of the evidence on the fashion-setting leadership of the courtesan class is instructive.

> New Orleans' white upper-class women directly copied clothing worn by its home-town prostitutes. Rose describes one madam, Countess Willie V. Piazza, as being an especially important influence on the fashions of respectable ladies in the city: . . . the "Countess ," who of course had no hereditary claim to such a title, wore a monocle, smoked Russian cigarettes in a two-foot ivory, gold and diamond holder, and favored a diamond choker around her slim neck. In contrast to Lulu White, Piazza could easily have "passed" for white. She was truly a fashion leader of her time, and many respectable matrons of New Orleans' first families attended the annual opening days at the Fair Grounds racetrack with their dressmakers in tow just to copy the outfits worn by Countess Willie and her girls.[35]

The courtesan class challenged status-quo fashion sensibility not only for outerwear, but also by promoting the rise of pretty and sexy lingerie. Tandberg notes that "perhaps because of the fashion leadership of the prostitute, the period between 1890 and 1914 is noted for its lavish and titillating underwear." Fashion writers of the time sought to break the association of dainty undergarments with the courtesan class. "'Respectable' women began to 'pick up the tricks of the trade,' but needed to rationalize their use of them."[36]

Tandberg explains the importance of hair and wigs in stimulating sexual interest. This is another area where courtesans were trendsetters. Tandberg notes that hair is not only a sexual symbol signifying femininity; it is also associated with young, virginal, unmarried women. "As early as the Roman period, bleached blond hair, much later adopted by Mae West, became the mark of the prostitute. Lulu White was not the only prostitute of the early 19th century to make her hair appear to be more abundant by wearing a wig."[37] Through her search of police files, Tandberg identified other District workers who wore wigs either as a beauty enhancement or to disguise their identities. The Million Dollar Baby Dolls and most certainly the groups that came after them wore blonde wigs, as travel writer Eleanor Early wrote in 1947.

PROBLEMATIC ASPECTS OF EARLY BABY DOLL MASKING

While much is made about Mardi Gras being the one day that people were free from social norms, the Million Dollar Baby Dolls freed themselves within the confines of race, sex, and class oppression to break gender norms each and every day. Mardi Gras was just that one day that they dressed together to make a scene and capitalize on the hustling behaviors that characterized their occupation and lifestyle.

New Orleans's fiscal fortune depended on the marketing of opportunities for sex across the color line, especially the indulgence of White male fantasies about the primitive sexuality of women of color.[38] The women who were "Baby Dolls, today and everyday," were central to that economy. In fact, Beatrice Hill bragged to Robert McKinney that the White sailors preferred the "brownies."[39] "See when them ships come in? That's when you made money. All them sailors wanted a brownie. 'Gimme a brownie,' they'd say. High yellers fared poorly less they got into them freakish shows when them sailors come along, but they did alright in their everyday bisness."

Promoting its reputation for sexual excess and permissiveness, the District was economically flush. Baby Dolls seized on opportunities to participate as entrepreneurs, prostitutes, and vocal members of their communities. As such, while many met terrible ends, others earned a living, and they established their own identities. Some even used their earnings to buy property and then used the courts to defend their rights to it. Misunderstood, devalued, and ignored by Whites and middle-class Blacks, these women formed a sisterhood; yet at the same time, they were committed to being almost completely unreliable and ungovernable, except to meet their own obligations to masking and dancing. For every Black woman prostitute that he dismissed as a "frustrated whore" in interview after interview, Robert McKinney could write with great detail and doting admiration about one woman's proud walk (e.g., Mary Davis)[40] or about another's undisputed authority among the residents of the rooming house she occupied. McKinney described Baby Doll Clara Belle as "virtually the boss of the neighborhood."[41] The Black women he interviewed were unashamed or, as he put it, "they were proud," and with that radically subversive attitude, they flipped Victorian conventions on their head.

There was a variety of reasons that a space existed for Black women to insert themselves into the new sexual economy and to display their profession flagrantly on Mardi Gras Day. Long a stronghold for the sale of light-skinned Black women as sexual slaves for White men,[42] the city had a tolerance for sex across the color line unmatched in other U.S. municipalities. As women who worked in the cribs and dance halls and plied their trade publicly (in the streets and doorways of rooming houses), they were already accustomed to performing in public. In addition, these Black women were part of a culture that encouraged street dancing for second-line funeral parades, which included the participation of women. Defiant women had a history of cross-dressing and appearing on public streets during Mardi Gras, braving the insults of the "respectable" classes, so the use of male behaviors such as cigar smoking, flinging money at men, and "bucking" up against their rivals should come as no surprise.

Baby Doll masking at Mardi Gras reinscribed the view that women were mere sexual toys for men. With short skirts, revealing halters, flirty behavior, and money in garters that everyone suspected was earned through prostitution, such a view would render them little more than "passive objects of a castrating male gaze."[43] The sensationalist writings of White men, some of whom observed the Baby Dolls in action and others who uncritically reproduced this view in their writings,[44] emphasized the women's jostling for the attention of the men in the Zulu parade or Big Chiefs of the Mardi Gras Indian gangs or any man with a dollar.

Black jazz musicians who interacted with the Baby Dolls from the early days of jazz until the 1970s were often quoted by White male writers in an indiscriminate and confusing way. One might emphasize the women's nude dancing while another might say that Baby Dolls were more than a little bawdy, but for fun purposes only. These men were from different generations, witnessing differing versions of Baby Doll masking groups.

These contradictory representations continue to the present. Even today, those in the Baby Boom generation recall their mothers and grandmothers warning them against the lewd and lascivious behavior evidenced by many a Baby Doll on Carnival Day. One New Orleanian, who spent Carnivals on Claiborne Avenue, recounted a colorful story of being teased by her mother if it appeared that she might misbehave. Her mother would threaten to mask as a Baby Doll and would playfully get her husband's consent. This struck terror in her daughter's heart since the Baby Dolls she saw would be drunk, and they would let loose.[45] In contrast, Mercedes Stevenson's mother did not object to her following the Baby Dolls around in her uptown neighborhood of circa late 1930s and 1940s. These women were known in the neighborhood as a fun-loving trio of friends who worked hard in their daily lives and hosted parties in their time off. Ms. Stevenson herself would go on to mask as a Baby Doll in the early 1970s. She has carried the spirit of her community's maskers for decades, before becoming the Big Queen of the Wild Tchoupitoulas Indian Gang, a position she continues to hold.[46]

BLACK WOMEN'S LIVES IN 1912

The year 1912 was not a good one for African American women. Women in general were without basic citizenship rights; they would not gain the right to vote until the Nineteenth Amendment was ratified in 1920. African American women were affected by laws that were meant to restrict their ability to become gainfully and respectfully employed. Sex and race discrimination easily dampened their aspirations and damaged their sense of self. With some notable exceptions, African American women in New Orleans had few educational opportunities and were corralled into low-paying and demoralizing work. The jobs available were mostly as washerwomen, servants in private homes, agricultural laborers, factory workers, and, from 1897 to 1917, legalized prostitution.

Beatrice Hill credited Leola Tate with having the organizational skills to establish their social and pleasure club. Census records reveal two Black women named Leola Tate in New Orleans around 1912. It is likely that neither is the Leola Tate of Hill's story. But one thing is probable; the life circumstances of the two Leola Tates could easily resemble those of the heroine of Hill's story.

The first Leola was estimated to have been born about 1895 and was twenty-five at the time of the 1920 census.[47] Her mother, Rosie (Rosa) Miller, was sixteen when she married Charles Tate, a man who worked as a laborer on the railroad. Rosie was not able to read or write.[48] Yet she managed to keep her large family together when Charles was no longer in the picture. (He was not included with them in the 1920 census). By 1920, each of Rosie's five adult children was working as a laborer. Leola was listed as a married woman, though no husband's name was recorded. She lived with her mother and her siblings, Charles, Allen, Louisa, and George, and her niece Albertine, age six, and Allen, her nephew, age five. Rosie was renting at 539 Franklin Street near Poydras in the Third Ward. The eldest, Charles, thirty-two, was a laborer in an auto factory; Allen (Aleck), twenty-two, labored under the direction of a contractor; Leola, twenty-five, and Louisa, eighteen, worked in a tobacco factory; and George, seventeen, worked in a market. The family's next-door neighbors, the Morisos, were Italian. They too were renters, and their household consisted of two married couples and the niece and brother-in-law of the Morisos, who were listed as head of the house. The Morisos could not read, write, or speak English. Mr. Moriso worked as a laborer on the levee, as did the other two men in the household. Near their home was a renter, sixty-year-old Sam Sing, an unmarried man originally from China and the owner of a laundry. Though he was not a citizen, he could read, write, and speak English. He lived with a boarder, twenty-four-year-old Isaac Bank, a Black male laborer and Louisiana native.

The 1930 census reveals that Charles Jr. was still living with his mother, who was no longer taking in laundry and did not list an occupation.[49] Seventeen-year-old Albertine was working at a factory as a pecan picker, and her father, Charles, listed his occupation as a roofer. Aleck was still attending school. Louisa seemed to have been a boarder with a married couple down the street from her mother. She was listed as single and with no occupation.

The second Leola Tate was born around 1908, and in 1930 she was married to twenty-four-year-old Henry Tate, who worked as a chauffeur for an undertaker. Twenty-two-year-old Leola was a servant in a private household. The couple lived at 1418 South Liberty Street. Though not to the extent of the neighborhood of the other Leola Tate a decade earlier, Leola and Henry's neighborhood was multiracial.

It is reasonable to assume that many of the Million Dollar Baby Dolls grew up in circumstances in which their mothers were illiterate and married young to men who may have also been illiterate. They had large families and were challenged to provide for them through labor-intensive jobs. Both parents were required to work to support their large families, though women could work from home by taking in laundry. In spite of the stresses, some single women managed to keep their families together and to see their children through to adulthood. Many lived in mixed-race neighborhoods and, though literacy rates were not high, there was an air of worldliness that could have been attained by close exposure to recent immigrant populations. It is likely that in 1912 women had no better prospects for employment than did their mothers and fathers and were destined to work at tedious, dead-end jobs outside the home that placed them at risk of sexual harassment. Wages were low, and rents could be high. A hand-to-mouth existence was almost guaranteed.

The 1930 census includes one Beatrice Hill who seemed to reflect the profile of the woman bearing that name who was interviewed by Robert McKinney in 1940. She lived at 454 South Liberty at the corner of Liberty and Perdido,[50] the heart of Black Storyville. She listed her age as thirty-five, and she was unable to read or write. She recorded the age of her first marriage to be fourteen and her employment as a housemaid for a private family.

The women who formed the Million Dollar Baby Dolls Social and Pleasure Club were already eroticized in the everyday course of their work in the District, but on Carnival, they re-eroticized themselves to mock and entice male and female spectators. What makes their original masking a challenge to the castrating male gaze of their patriarchal milieu was their aim to get the attention not of men but of a group of women that they held up as rivals and competitors. The Baby Dolls were part of a culture in which competitions among artistic groups were common. For example, it was commonplace to see the leading member of a jazz band publicly guide his group in a competition against another jazz band at a street intersection to see who was "king." The Mardi Gras Indians took rivalry to a new level as they actually settled old scores on Carnival in their masked attire, guns concealed by elaborate feathered cloaks. Danny Barker recalled that two women singers, Esther Bigeou, an accomplished singer of Creole songs, and Lizzie Miles, were competitors. That they came from different parts of the city only heightened their desire to outdo each other. Seventh Ward resident Esther Bigeou and Sixth Ward resident Lizzie Miles would perform in venues where each had brought her own "gang" who rooted for them as fans of prizefighters do for their champions. In addition to their entourages and their artistic repertoires, they carried with them an array of beautiful gowns and would change between performances.[51] Both had mothers who were seamstresses, and so each woman's attire was elegant and their competition extended to style as well.

The original intent of the Baby Dolls was solely about female spectatorship. Men were not the object of their gaze. Rather, their aim, clearly and colorfully stated, was to outdo and impress another group of Black women they defined as competitors, a group that in their estimation had unearned privilege due to their ability to work "downtown."

BLACK WOMEN'S LEGAL AND CULTURAL RESISTANCE

These women gained their headstrong attitudes and proven leadership abilities through their daily interactions with patterns of domination and subordination, both in their relationships with their male lovers and in the exploitation encountered in their work environments. They were gained as well through their routine negotiations of inequality as women to men, as poor to rich, as Black to White, and as disenfranchised to enfranchised. They paid a high price for creating even this modicum of pleasure for themselves. The price included venereal diseases, high-risk abortions, drug addiction and alcoholism, homelessness, and both domestic and workplace violence. But it is not certain that in 1912 they would have escaped these risks or fared any better if they had not been working in the District. Despite the challenges, they carved out a niche of empowerment that combined the annual opportunity for free expression with the African American tradition of creating live art. If masking is about self-expression, what were the maskers trying to tell us? Black maskers impart the following message to adoring fans and mystified tourists: They are beautiful and good looking. They are tough and can survive. They are valuable beyond all measure and, in a society that discriminated against them, this was an important statement. They belonged to a community of people who saw them as important. They inspired others to feel joy and to be happy.

Leola Tate, Beatrice Hill, and Clara Belle Moore—the original Million Dollar Baby Dolls—were not an anomaly among Black women in the commercial sex industry in refusing to silence themselves or to retreat to the margins of their society to live in shame and disgrace. They rebuffed pressures to be submissive, helpless women as the prevailing social norms required for "respectable women."

In 1897 the New Orleans City Council passed an ordinance that would serve to segregate women in the population based on their occupation. Ordinance number 13032 C.S. created a vice district. A later ordinance that year (number 13845) created one in the Perdido and Gravier streets area but held it in abeyance. Both districts were located within largely African American but mixed-race neighborhoods. Nor were these the only red-light districts to have been imposed on majority African American communities. The red-light district in Crowley, Louisiana, located in Acadia Parish, was created amidst collective opposition of African Americans and White reformers. Crowley's red-light district was placed in the Black section of the city derogatively known as "Coontown." Although the city had established a school for Black children, once the Crowley Ordinance went into effect, brothels sat right across the street from the school.[52]

The Storyville ordinance aimed to regulate where any "public prostitute or woman notoriously abandoned to lewdness" could "occupy, inhabit, live, or sleep in any house, room, or closet." Storyville was bounded by Customhouse (now Iberville) and St. Louis and North Basin (now North Saratoga) and North Robertson streets.[53] A second district was created several blocks away in a heavily populated African American neighborhood bounded by Perdido and Gravier and Basin and Locust streets.[54] This second district was held in abeyance, but "vice" flourished there between 1897 and 1917 and well into the midcentury.

Several blocks away from "Black Storyville" was the larger vice district, aggressively marketed to the nation as a sexual playground. The District had become famous for its large mansions, wealthy madams, sex shows, sex across the color line (especially with light-skinned Black women, who called themselves octoroons), music, and gambling. Several light-skinned Black women ran successful brothels, presiding over a workforce of sex laborers, musicians, and servants. These women owned swaths of property inside the District and sometimes beyond. One such woman was Willie Piazza.

Facing mounting pressure from reformers and the federal government in 1917, in their attempt to prevent the closing of Storyville, the New Orleans City Council made a stab at cleaning up the District, not by closing the brothels but by banning women of color from living there. Ordinance 4118 C.C.S. was passed on February 7 in an attempt to racially segregate Storyville. "Colored" prostitutes, including light-skinned women like Lulu White and Willie Piazza, and dark-skinned women such as Carrie Gross, who enjoyed few of the luxuries of her lighter-skinned contemporaries, along with many others were ordered to move into Black Storyville. Piazza would not be able to live and run her business out of property she owned on 317 Basin Street; ironically, the area she and the others were being relocated to was already overpopulated.

On March 1, 1917, police officers sought to force Piazza, her employees, and boarders out of the house she owned. Piazza's attorney filed an injunction to prevent the city from enforcing the ordinance. The Second Recorder's Court found Piazza guilty and fined her for every day she would not vacate the premises. Piazza appealed to the Louisiana Supreme Court, which "annulled, avoided and reversed" the lower court's decision.[55] In spite of her reputation, and being a Black woman at that, she won her case. She and Lulu White inspired other Black women to file lawsuits. Over twenty Black women sought refuge in the courts.

The court found that the city could issue ordinances to close houses of prostitution but had overstepped its bounds when it attempted to order segregated housing arrangements. As long as they were not plying their trade, prostitutes, the court decided, were entitled to live where they pleased. The owners of homes, even Black public women, could rent to whomever they saw fit as long as those boarders and renters were conducting themselves within the law.

While Piazza and other African American women waged their battle for property in the courts, the Million Dollar Baby Dolls staged their battles for identity and representation in the court of public opinion. In both cases, the women set precedents and left an enduring legacy. The gender performativity of the Million Dollar Baby Dolls not only transgressed the social norms for women; it was also a disavowal of heteronormativity. Middle-class Black women in the Victorian era aspired to a standard of "uplifting the race," involving such activities as marriage, childrearing, chastity, and making contributions to the public good.[56] But the women in the District were outcasts and as such they took liberties to renounce gender scripts that they could not conform to anyway. Their masculinized self-assertion was seen by reformers and city fathers as fostering a crisis of civilization. To save society, the women—not the men who sought their services—were viewed as needing to be residentially segregated, their movements circumscribed, and their behaviors monitored.

From the perspective of reformers and city fathers, women acting in ways that were unfeminine were disruptive to White male hegemonic rule. As such, the women in the District were considered bizarre, unattractive, unpredictable, dirty, and disgusting. They were referred to as "public women" or "women notoriously abandoned to lewdness." They were deemed undeserving of attention unless they could be reprimanded harshly. And while they were largely unseen, except to be scapegoated as an immoral element of society, their solidarity and strong leadership qualities, which challenged the gender-polarized norms of separate spheres for men and women, were unremarked upon by reformers of the day and unappreciated by all. The Million Dollar Baby Doll Social and Pleasure Club resisted the pressures to behave with idealized feminine passivity. The Baby Dolls took feminine objects and used them in the reverse of what they had come to signify.[57] The baby doll dresses offered a "tongue in cheek" or a "ha ha feminine" performance.[58] When they masked, the Million Dollar Baby Dolls disrupted the gender script of female submissiveness, dependence, and chastity. Through performing gender "buffoonery," they created a safe space for cross-dressing men. Men also masked in the short satin dresses with bonnets and bloomers and paraded with the women.

Gender identities are not naturally occurring phenomena, but must be carefully maintained. They must be asserted and reasserted, spoken, performed, and reinscribed on the body.[59] As they pretended to be "real" babies, these women offered a critique that femininity was not biological, but was instead a social construct. Their aggression, flirting, bucking, and competing postures challenged notions of gender authenticity. This is a legacy that has endured in this live art form.

IN THEIR OWN VOICE? THE MILLION DOLLAR BABY DOLL TRADITION OF SINGING AND CHANTING

Speaking of the New Orleans of his boyhood, about 1909, Danny Barker recalled that "all kinds of music" could be heard "all day."[60] A cappella singing by street vendors, organ grinding, brass bands jazzing it up for merchants advertising a product or the opening of their businesses, and relatives practicing their instruments at home were part of everyday life. "You heard all kinds of people passing by singing." Just the sound of a band would evoke excitement, and people would rush to join the parade, only to discover it was "just people carrying a big sign, one holding the back pole saying 'Bargain at Smith's Butcher Shop,' 'Bargain at Vincent Domingo's.'" Musical talent seemed to be ubiquitous. Some street peddlers "had beautiful voices, and they could sing what they had. Sing a sad song, or say anything foolish" such as, "Hey, mademoiselle," "*Venez ici,*" by which Barker meant, "Come see Sam and me." Those in various occupations found ways to market their wares and services by displaying distinguishing features. The junk man, for example, "had them bells he would ring. Them cowbells they used to put on a cow's neck."

Black women wearing wide-hooped skirts secured their baskets of goods on their heads. "It would be the blackberry lady or the strawberry lady or the pie lady." And there were elderly women that sold *calas.* "*Cala* is a rice cake. It had rice and flour, and it looks like a round doughnut, like a brown biscuit. Everybody had a song." Not only did these passersby have a song, they also had a story. "The junk man, he had a story. The milkman, he didn't say nothing. The ice man, he had a story. He'd tell you, selling ice."

There are other traditions that influenced the Million Dollar Baby Dolls' music making. These have to do with ritual, namely, the Mardi Gras Indian song and chanting traditions. Another involves the rise of bawdy songs as part of the jazz canon and the African American word game called "playing the dozens."[61] Chanting consists of words and sounds that are either spoken or sung, often to simple melodies. The Mardi Gras Indians have a well-developed repertoire that accompanies their "practices" or weekly meetings of a neighborhood-based "tribe" to prepare for their coming out in costume for Mardi Gras each year. Jason Berry noted that Indian chants are accompanied by tambourines, sticks, and bottles, but not drums. Over time, these groups developed a body of chants whose aim is the lauding of the achievements of Indians and praising the spirit of rebellion.[62] Popular Indian chants include "two poackaway," which stands for "get out of the way," or "jock-a-mo fee-no ai na-ne," which references the meeting of tribes.[63]

The Black Spiritual churches of New Orleans, founded and shaped by Leafy Anderson, incorporated several spiritual dimensions, from Catholicism to Spiritualism to the symbolic healing aspects of Haitian and West African religious practices. Central to Anderson's teachings was the compelling presence of "spirit guides" such as Black Hawk, the legendary Sauk Indian leader in the midwestern United States. Spiritual churches would have celebrations of such guides. Jason Berry recalled his participant observation in this way. During the course of the ceremony the congregation was led through chants to the Indian. They emphasized the role of Black Hawk as a watchman who would fight their battles and who "melded into a positive theme of reinforcement a common struggle for solidarity."[64]

When African American anthropologist Irene Diggs, who studied music and dance in Cuba, evaluated the influence of African culture on the people of the African Diaspora, she highlighted the special nature of the African cultural innovation that had endured the middle passage.[65] Culture was developed in Africa and in the Diaspora in ways best captured by terms like democracy, communalism, creative consultation, and collective elaboration. This was true of the 1950s-era Cuba that Diggs studied and remains true today among African American maskers in New Orleans.

To express themselves, African American Mardi Gras masking groups use costuming, parading, the music of brass bands, singing, chanting, and clapping. And they use dance. Diggs observed that "poetry, music, and dance are frequently united and with certain reservations, the music of Africa is the music of dance." Moreover, "African people dance for pleasure and sorrow, for birth and death, for hate and love, for prosperity, for religious motives, and just to pass time." And it was not so much that the music inspired the dance, but that the dance inspired the music.

African American women who originated the Baby Doll masking practice were dancers, and not only for paid employment. They were young adults in the historical era of the "New Woman"[66] in which women were beginning to strive for personal autonomy. Dancing the jazz offered them a way to express their independence. Eventually, each neighborhood had its own group of Baby Dolls. They sang, clapped their hands, and danced with abandon on the streets as they walked around during Carnival.

Diggs taught that the role of song in African and African Diaspora culture was beyond entertainment alone: "They sing their jokes, their satire, hopes and disillusions. In song, they conserve their history, traditions, fables and mythology. Songs are frequently 'editorials,' critical daily life chronicles, or news commentaries."[67] Baby Dolls are on record for parading "in groups chanting in Creole patois over and over again. 'Aye aye mo pé allé quitté Hey, hey, hey [I'm going to quit my job].'"[68] They also celebrated their own bodies, chanting, "I got good boody, yeah, yeah!"

Like the African American actors who played stereotyped characters in early Hollywood films, the Baby Dolls have been largely dismissed from serious academic discussion. Why did certain songs become popular among various Baby Doll groups? One problem is that the majority of their songs were of a bawdy nature, and there is simply a paucity of information regarding these songs and chants. Another critical factor is the absence of Black researchers.

For example, compare the work of African Americans in constructing the history of Blacks in Louisiana in the Dillard University Negro project of the WPA era to *Gumbo Ya-Ya,* a book that downplayed Louisiana's heinous slave-owning past and presented the bygone era as a paradise for those who lived through it. Robert McKinney was the only African American writer collecting data that found its way to *Gumbo Ya-Ya* and hence he was instructed to collect information on African Americans at the margins of New Orleans society. While it is a wonderful idea to include those who are pushed out of the mainstream, it is a problem because it constructs a skewed representation that supports an argument in favor of Black moral turpitude and intellectual inferiority. Ronnie Clayton provided a trenchant comparison of the two projects: "While *Gumbo Ya-Ya* tended to portray blacks in a stereotype role of buffoons, the Dillard writers intended to describe Whites in a jocular fashion."[69]

A further problem was that Blacks were found to be more expressive to the Black interviewers than to White project interviewers.[70] Indeed, during his visits McKinney was often accompanied by White co-interviewers and photographers. McKinney's typed notes were filled with his own and his interviewees' comments about the presence of Whites: "As soon as the camera-man and his ala Hollywood constituents reached Poydras and Saratoga streets the Baby Dolls jumped on them excitedly attempting to sell their wares. They broke to the white faces first because there is peculiar belief among Negro prostitutes that white men are not as tight as Negros."[71]

Just like the Black actors in early Hollywood films who infused their stereotyped roles with a creative vision and were dismissed, ignored, derided, and publicly scolded by Black activists, the Baby Dolls were accomplished in a unique art form. From Stepin Fetchit and Louise Beavers to Sidney Poitier and Whoopi Goldberg, the point is not that they played stereotyped roles, but rather what they achieved within these roles. Film critic Donald Bogle notes that such "actors have elevated kitch or trash and brought to it arty qualities, if not pure art itself."[72] Bogle makes the case that "the past had to be contended with. It had to be defined, recorded, reasoned with, and interpreted."[73] He noted further that ignoring stereotypical performances neglects "the strength of performance and . . . denied black America a certain cultural heritage."[74] In 1940 Robert McKinney expressed similar thoughts about the importance of Baby Doll masking: "A large crowd was on hand, around Poydras and Saratoga Streets, the cradle of dope, to watch the Baby Dolls do their stuff amid a 'glory' that is somewhat shameful to an aristocratic eye but is good entertainment."[75]

African Americans enjoyed coming up with euphemisms for sex. "Jass" first referred to sexual intercourse and then to music that invited men and women to dance together in sexually suggestive ways. The words "boogie woogie," "jelly roll," and "swing" were all infused with sexual connotations. Speaking of sex in displacement onto unusual objects, people, and places generated humor among listeners. Ribald and bawdy songs were used as commentary on non-sexual matters of urgent concern to people who shared similar values. Euphemism thus became satire, a form of expressive culture that African American music, chanting, and dance excelled at conveying.

Historian Lawrence Levine wrote that "no inquiry into the consciousness and inner resources of black Americans can ignore the content and structure of Afro- American humor." Playing the dozens, also known as signifying or woofing, refers to a verbal sparring match in which insults to one's relatives, especially to one's mother, would defeat the opponent if he or she couldn't muster a better response. Levine reports that Buddy Bolden and his band members when arriving at the bandstand would play the dozens with lines like "Is your mother still in the district catchin' tricks?" Black scholars active in the Black power and civil rights movements identified girls as being especially good with the dozens.[76]

The Baby Dolls used their made-up lyrics in keeping with the signifying tradition. The Million Dollar Baby Dolls had standard songs and chants, including a few crowd pleasers. "Sure, we use to sing. . . . What we sang? We sang, 'When the Sun goes down,'"[77] and "When the saints come marching through I want to be in that number. I'll tell you another song we used to sing that everybody liked." That song is quoted in full in McKinney's typed transcript of the interview.[78] The song was called "You Dirty Man" with the lyric, "Your momma don't wear no drawers." It was set to a popular vaudeville tune. The lyrics are a combination of braggadocio about the woman's sexual prowess, sexual endurance, and ability to sexually enslave a lover. It is at the same time a critique of the haughty man who seeks her favors and would then dare to judge her as a "public woman." In a refrain that refers to the man's mother not wearing any "drawers,"[79] the lyrics point out the hypocrisy of a man judging a woman for being sexually free when his own mother may be the same way. In the hands of the Million Dollar Baby Dolls, it is a scathing critique of the sexual double standard and the dichotomy of good versus bad women. The song/chant appropriates the style of the dozens: "Hey you dirty [man]," the chant goes, "Your momma . . . !"

EYEWITNESS ACCOUNT: MAURICE MARTINEZ

Maurice M. Martinez was born in New Orleans to Mildred Mouton Martinez and Harold Theodore Martinez. His mother owned and operated the first nursery school for Black children in the city. Martinez's nursery school educated generations of middle-class children including such luminaries as the city's second Black mayor, Sidney Barthelemy; Liberty Bank president Alden McDonald; and former Orleans Parish School Board member Gail Glapion. Mildred founded the school to shield her son from the racism of their time and to make education available to Black children who were being neglected because they could not enter White nursery schools.[80] In 1976, Maurice produced the first documentary on the Mardi Gras Indian masking tradition, titled *The Black Indians of New Orleans.* This film explores the song, dances, costuming, and performativity of the tradition along with the influences from the Yoruba of West Africa and Native Americans.[81] I will conclude this chapter with Martinez's recollections about the Baby Dolls:

What can I tell you about the Baby Dolls? Many of them carried that reputation throughout the year. "There goes Ms. Baby Doll!" They always seemed to have time to stop, no matter how rushed they were. "How you doing child?" "Hello honey." "I remember you. How's your mama and them?" They valued the interpersonal relationship. They valued people over things. We didn't have many things because of rampant poverty among African Americans.

There were two unemployment boards: one for whites and one for blacks. The one for blacks was for labor and low-wage jobs. The board for whites was for white collar jobs. Some of the guys in the army were teachers like me and they were telling me they were getting paid in the summer. I went down to the board and said I am here to see about getting paid. I am a GI and so they gave me a typing test. It was blatant rejection to your face and it was not uncommon to hear "Who let them niggers in here?" That goes right through you. You are trying to do the right thing, preparing yourself, studying hard, even taking up a weapon to defend the county, and you come back and hear that. That's why I am proud of those with the courage to take it to the streets in costume, like the walking groups such as the Baby Dolls and the Mardi Gras Indians. They had a spirit that refused to be crushed.

The more risqué, raunchy groups came from Tremé from what I can gather. Those from the Seventh Ward didn't wear the garter with the money, but they were still out there singing and enjoying themselves. Those in the Seventh Ward carried sticks, or it could have been a walking cane. It was useful if someone comes up to you. They were classy. They carried elaborate pursues and black patent-leather tap shoes.

In the male social and pleasure clubs, there was a subtle organization. The first line to hit the streets was a guard, and there would be four or five just moving along and one would be carrying drinks. Behind them would be the first masker in a dyed hat, orchid-colored suit, and alligator shoes; followed by the banner announcing who they are. "Look who is coming." If you watch the second line, you could see people who were not masked. These were huge guys who served as protection. Same thing with the Baby Dolls. They had protection. You wouldn't notice it; but if you go in and try to touch one of them you would be in big trouble. Same thing with the Indians, their protection carried the guns. If they needed it, it would come to them. The Indians carried decorated shot guns. There were skirmishes back then.

Every group that seemed disorganized was well organized. They moved along a route according to their feelings. For Zulus, one float would be at a barroom and the other float would be two blocks away. Things would be falling off. But there was organization in the disorganization. It was not organized according to a time schedule or route. For the Indian, if he decided he wanted to go this way or that he would and you were lucky if you could find him. That is a freedom of spirit that comes out of that; a spirit of joy.

Every year at Carnival, at a time when we were told that we were Mongoloids and inferior human beings, Allison "Tootie" Montana, the Baby Dolls and all others in costumes came out and said, don't listen to the crap, look at me, come and see my beauty and rejoice with me. "I may empty your bedpans all year long, but today, I am the prettiest thing you are going to see." It was a manifestation of pride and what I really intended to be. It made us forget for a moment the evil, the rejection, the job discrimination, and we could enjoy life.

My grandmother knew all the Baby Dolls. She made *calas* and they would come to get a drink, eat fried rice cakes, and when they saw one another they spoke in French. They sang and they were happy to see each other. When the children would come up, they would switch to English and you learned to be profane in two languages.

Baby Dolls were pretty women with pretty smiles. They were women who brought fun to communities that were suffering financially. They were not afraid to party and to get down. They flaunted their inner spirit against convention and against conformity to conservative ideology. They sang songs like "When the Saints Go Marching In," and they imitated the vaudeville circuit's use of standard show tunes turned risqué. In New Orleans, when movie theaters changed reels at intermission, there would be a stage show and beautiful ladies in short dresses would dance to a rhythm. The drummer was sending them a message, "Do you have good booty?" When he hit the bass drum, they would reply, "Yeah man." They would get down and shake all the way down to the floor. A lot of that was carried to the street with the Baby Dolls.

The group that I remember with Alfred Glapion, Arthur Hubbard, and others who made up the kazoo band was a lady who was *the* Baby Doll. Her name was Ms. Lapersol,[82] and she was in the Seventh Ward with her friends Ophelia and Rita. They were located on Villere near St. Bernard Avenue right around the corner from Big Chief "Tootie" Montana, and they came out from that area. Everybody belonged to a social and pleasure club or a mutual aid society. This was how we shared resources with one another and how people survived in an impoverished society that discriminated in jobs and professions. She was a member of two prominent groups in the Seventh Ward: the Original Paramount Club and the Orchid Girls. From that group those who wanted to be Baby Dolls would come out; about eight or nine of them. They sang the "Saints" with the kazoo band, but what they liked best was a song composed by the black gay musician, Tony Jackson, "Pretty Baby." That was their theme song; they loved it. And as they came from one block to the next block, they would repeat the performance because you would have a new audience in that block.

What did they do? They brought joy and love. When you look at the lyrics of "Pretty Baby," you can hear that. They brought smiles. I will never forget looking up at this woman and she had on pink silk panties. Most of them had stockings and bloomers, but she had her legs out. She had on a pink garter with dollar bills and patent leather shoes.[83] Some had taps, and when they hit streets that had hard surfaces, they would tap dance. . . . She came sashaying up to me. . . . She looked down at me and started singing "Pretty Baby, cuddle with me." It made me feel so good inside. It brought out *élan vital,* the vital spirit that is within. . . .

She was a bombshell and that is what made me want to go out into the streets and look at the culture of my people. She had an infectious smile that penetrated. It is the kind of smile you get after you have a good orgasm. That kind of smile can carry you anywhere. It is an infectious, self-contained smile. You see it in my film the *Mardi Gras Indians*. . . . There is something in that that unlocks the strength and fortitude of black culture. They had the ability to laugh at agony and pain and to enjoy that inner feeling of having made something out of nothing in spite of the overwhelming odds of rejection.

. . . Everybody knew them. Some say they were tough women; but they were party girls. There is the story of one Creole woman whose husband did not want her to be a Baby Doll. She found a way. She sent him on his way early Carnival morning; then she snuck over to her girlfriend's house, dressed, and went with them. In her last year masking, Ms. Lapersol came out in velvet, velvet buttons, and fur trim. They had lace trim on the satin. They would wear long underwear because it would be cold. They had the bonnets, rattles, pacifiers, and baby bottles. . . . These costumes were handmade, and they put the petticoats underneath to make the skirts stand out.

One year this same group, that had men masked as policemen, came out dressed as women. You had Baby Dolls and men dressed as women, and they went around to Big Rip and he had on a diaper with yellow mustard as if he had pooped. They had a ball. Singing and enjoying each other's company and celebrating life.[84]

A New Group of Baby Dolls Hits the Streets

The [Zulu] King's float winds through the streets, followed by black and white. Many of the Negroes are masked. Most of the women are Baby Dolls, with blonde wigs and white faces. Many of the men are Indians.
    —*Eleanor Early,* A New Orleans Holiday, *1947*

• •

MARDI GRAS REVELRIES in antebellum New Orleans consisted of neighbors and friends hosting private and public balls and masquerade parties in their own homes, as well as taking part in informal street processions. Enslaved Africans and free people of color participated in Mardi Gras masking. Whether through dancing in Congo Square or through promenading on Chartres Street to visit "fancy stores," or putting on "grotesque" disguises and wandering in merriment through the streets, on Carnival, Black people participated. Some may have appropriated the fete for religious purposes, while others may have used the celebration as an opportunity to resist social limitations.[1] Women had much more license to participate in Carnival activities than they would later. Notably through the practice of the quadroon balls, free women of color attended masked balls where White men, would-be-suitors, swelled the halls with their presence. Monique Guillory's analysis of the system of *plaçage* and its attendant practice of the quadroon balls shows how free women of color seized control of the commodification of their own bodies to set their own prices. They were so successful that White women tried to "pass" as women of color to secure successful men to take care of them as lifetime partners or attended, risking their reputations, to check on their husbands. In her fascinating interpretation, Guillory attributes the success of the quadroon women not to their beauty but to their "mastery of whiteness." These women were highly educated, could speak French, and often their mothers were property owners or successful in business. Their business acumen may have developed, she speculates, through the sale of their own bodies as their first, but most important, commodity.[2]

Beginning in 1857, the laissez-faire Creole style of Mardi Gras was threatened. White men from non-Creole backgrounds saw an opportunity to assert their power and control over a public they believed they were losing control over due to issues of "states' rights" regarding slavery. The first krewe, an exclusive club who charged themselves with nighttime street parades and dominating the celebration with their social events, was founded and was to be followed by many others. The all-White, all-male, all-monied Mardi Gras krewes staged parades, held elite private balls complete with *tableaux,* and regulated the participation of women of their class by requiring them to attend these functions unmasked, while the members of the krewe were masked. Their greatest public statement came through taking possession of the street at night in a formal parade that consisted of themed floats and masked riders, purportedly informing the masses of great European literature and world mythology told in a way that highlighted their own superiority and refinement. Middle- and upper-class women began to have diminished opportunity to mask playfully on Mardi Gras and at associated events. Rather than grotesque masking, they began to wear stock character costumes and, eventually, the appropriate attire became evening wear. Women's grotesque carnival costumes such as fabric male genitals hidden under flaps they might display to onlookers were especially threatening to social norms because, as Carolyn Ware notes, such practices afforded women the opportunity to "step into this unladylike role playing" and "provide[d] another vehicle for challenging ideals of decorum and beauty."[3]

According to Karen Leathem, women's masking held so much power that men felt threatened.[4] Once masked, women could set up, trick, and test the fidelity and respectable behavior of husbands, brothers, and neighbors. In time, masking and class status became associated. It was observed in newspapers of the early twentieth century that only common people masked. Once the "better" class of womenreached adolescence, they turned in their play costume for fashionable attire. Black women aspiring to respectability followed suit.

These acts changed Mardi Gras traditions, relegating the working classes and Blacks to mere spectator status during nighttime parades and to being labeled as "promiscuous maskers," meaning "common." But krewe members' attempts were not altogether successful. Women who worked in the legalized prostitution industry and women who earned their own incomes from the professions, such as doctors, were able to take to the streets, often in men's clothing.

A notable example can be found in Robert Tallant's *Mardi Gras.* He wrote that among the thirty thousand visitors to Carnival in 1870 was the first woman surgeon in the U.S. military, Dr. Mary E. Walker. She was reported to be "'disgusted at how out-Heroed' she was by women from Basin Street and other red-light districts, who like the famous doctor, were on the streets in male attire."[5] People don't necessarily "change" their personalities to accommodate Carnival; they appropriate Carnival as a vehicle to express an aspect of their everyday identity. Dr. Walker regularly dressed in men's clothing. Both Dr. Walker and the women from the red-light district can be said to have been upholding their reputations rather than striving to act with decorum.

The gender landscape was changing. The loosening of Victorian mores, women's demands for education and the vote, their leadership in reform movements, and their participation in labor movements served as a major impetus for the return of women to street masking in the early twentieth century. At the same time, in spite of aggressive legal opposition in New Orleans and elsewhere, legal segregation based on race had been instituted throughout the city and the nation as a whole. Disenfranchised "revelers invested broader political and social meanings in the frolicsome play, even if it was some inchoate sense of who could claim public space. On the streets of carnival, men and women acted out the ramifications of gender relations in the public sphere."[6]

While upper-class women largely remained passive observers of Carnival parades, tucked securely away on balconies, women without connections to property owners were braving the dangerous streets, which brought them uncomfortably close to male strangers who were not at all averse to making sexual assumptions and even approaches, overt and covert. Women could mitigate their risk by not wearing masked attire, for masking was associated with loose morals. Prostitutes, Leathem concluded, were threatening to society because they signaled that gender roles were in flux and that women did not have to be bound by family or propriety to survive. What's worse for city fathers was their fear that, if White women and Black men masked, Jim Crow was more of a challenge to uphold. Interracial sex would be more than possible as maskers passed for their socially constructed opposite race or gender. Masked "respectable" women could intermingle with prostitutes while watching parades on Canal Street, or worse, they would venture into Storyville to witness what they believed their male kin and husbands could see.

White men fought back using costuming and blackface. Noting the backlash, Leathem wrote that the men marched in clubs wearing "mammy" outfits and masked as "wenches and other grotesque images of African American women."[7] They lampooned the Zulu Social Aid and Pleasure Club with a themed float titled "Originators of the Tango" with riders in blackface and performing simian movements. They made fun of suffragists and club women by "waddling" down the street in hobble skirts. In another themed float called "Modern Evil," the men depicted "scantily gowned maidens" in modern attire with their "x-ray" features.

Nevertheless, by 1910 there were women of all races and classes who engaged in raucous behavior at Mardi Gras. With the introduction of cabarets around 1910, women were coming into social contact with those who daily defied propriety. New Orleans boasted a "Tango Belt" close to the District that was a favorite dance spot for even the social elite such as professors from Newcomb College, the women's higher-education institution. Popular dances like the tango caused outrage among moral authorities. One minister decried that "daylight" was not being seen between dancers.[8] Leathem amusingly noted that one could hardly distinguish whether the dancer in costume performing the turkey trot was from Newcomb or Storyville.

Leathem concluded that as women hid their identities, they exposed their bodies, some in imitation of the prostitutes. Pushing the boundaries of respectability, some openly confronted dowagers of New Orleans with an acrobatics performance in short skirts tumbling to the sounds of a jazz band. Others behaved with abandon in rough salons. Fashionable women transgressed in good hotels by putting one foot on the brass rail of the bar; others went out in clingy attire with whips to fend off aggressors.

Three popular groups of Black women started parading during the Progressive Era. Of those, the Baby Dolls developed and sustained the most notorious reputation. Speaking of a 1947 Mardi Gras, Robert Tallant reported:

The Baby Dolls, the Gold Diggers, and the Zigaboos are groups of women maskers, loosely knitted together, who, like the Zulus, have become traditional parts of the Negro Mardi Gras. The Gold Diggers usually travel through the streets with male companions, who dress in masculine costumes that match those worn by the girls. The Baby Dolls and the Zigaboos always start out alone, but they never end the day that way.

. . . Baby Dolls possess a keen affection for Mardi Gras, and a lot of thought and planning goes into their costumes and make-up. To be a Baby Doll they are supposed to look as innocent as possible, which may be accepted as a perfect example of altering one's personality, so they make their little skirts and bloomers out of chaste pink or virginal blue, the skirts pleated. They wear bloomers trimmed with ruffles and little bows. They wear waists or halters to match and bonnets that tie demurely beneath their chins. Their dusky faces, framed by long corkscrew curls of every shade, are heavily roughed and powdered. Some wear pink and blue socks, but most prefer long hose held up on their dark thighs with flashy, ruffled garters.

The Zigaboos are not quite so wicked a group and are not necessarily members of the same profession. They wear brief trunks and halters and fancy hats and often carry canes, [which] they use to effect when strutting through the streets. They walk "raddy," too, and are great favorites with Negro men, especially the Zulus, who have a fine time calling out to them from the floats and occasionally deserting the parade for a few minutes of dancing or very public love-making. Throughout the day the Zigaboos pick up men and leave them, visit the bars and the night clubs that are always open. Like the Baby Dolls, they are usually drunk with sherry, gin and love by dark, and are not alone.[9]

One of the few existing artistic renderings, perhaps the only one, of the Baby Dolls was done by John McCrady. McCrady was born in 1911 and spent his formative years in rural Mississippi and Louisiana. Most of the work for which he is best known can be described by his charge from the Guggenheim Foundation "to paint the life and faith of the Southern Negro."[10] During his time, his work was considered by some Whites to be a portrait, and a sensitive one at that, of the everyday life of African Americans, especially those in rural areas. But African Americans

"Negro Maskers," drawing by John McCrady. From Ralph Wickiser, Caroline Durieux, and John McCrady, *Mardi Gras Day* (New York: Henry Holt, 1948). Reproduced courtesy Blake McCrady Woods and the McCrady Estate.

"A group starts out for the day," drawing by John McCrady. From *Mardi Gras Day*. Reproduced courtesy Blake McCrady Woods and the McCrady Estate.

apparently saw his work as patronizing, resulting in a scathing critique that interrupted his depictions of African Americans and shifted his focus. Nevertheless, his "Negro Maskers" appeared in the 1948 book *Mardi Gras Day,* by artists Ralph Wickiser, Caroline Durieux, and John McCrady. Each artist contributed a series of drawings capturing scenes of Carnival festivities. Though he did not title the work "the Baby Dolls," it is an unmistakable representation of one of the three groups. His description bears this out: "Five Negroes, led by a masked woman, are going to see the Zulu parade even if they aren't in it. One passes his hat. They will get paid for their fun."[11]

McCrady uses himself and his family to offer a drawing with a larger community context. In his work titled "A group starts out for the day," nine revelers emerge from a shotgun house,[12] a home that McCrady owned and lived in with his wife on Palmyra Street. Two are masked as a devil and an angel, while two others, similarly dressed, are masked as Cyrano de Bergerac.[13] McCrady himself with his daughter Tucker and her cousin Kalma pose for a photograph. McCrady writes that one of the group yells, "Hurry up! We'll miss Zulu."[14] The family still owns the home, according to McCrady's grandson Blake Woods.[15]

THE SPREAD OF THE BABY DOLL MASKING PRACTICE

The Million Dollar Baby Dolls have come to embody the entire masking phenomenon. But they were just the beginning, and not the whole of the Baby Doll tradition. We can only speculate about the timing of their cultural impact on women in New Orleans. No one knows when Baby Doll masking crossed over and entered the mainstream African American community's Mardi Gras tradition. As difficult as it is to locate an exact date for the beginning of the Baby Doll practice, I settled on the development of the tradition during the founding years of Zulu and the Black Indian organizing because the founding members of these groups knew each other and were negotiating their public presences. Beatrice Hill emphatically stated that Johnny Metoyer, a founding member of the Zulus, wanted the Baby Dolls to become part of that group, but she rejected the offer, preferring to have her own gang.[16] This struggle for visibility and independent identity was undertaken by both men and women and exemplifies Sherrie Tucker's point that "jazz participation became a way of being modern, of participating in new musical forms, new technologies (such as radio, motor vehicle travel), and new gender possibilities at once. These different relationships held by women of jazz in New Orleans co-existed in close proximity facilitated by migration (both out and in), travel, religious diversity, ethnic diversity (and changing definitions, identifications and legal restrictions)."[17]

But exactly when the Baby Doll masking tradition entered mainstream Black culture no one can know for sure. Miriam Batiste Reed believes the heyday of her mother's masking was in the late 1930s. Born in 1927, Miriam has memories of her mother's masking back to when Miriam was eight, around 1935. Several things are clear: Black women's participation in the District had continued since the close of the formal vice district in 1917, and women from this occupational group continued to mask on Mardi Gras as Baby Dolls. What was also true was that many other groups of women who offered support services to that group of Baby Dolls, such as being their laundresses, were in close interaction with these women, especially about issues of dress and style, and they also masked as Baby Dolls with their own husbands, friends, and neighbors.

Moreover, men had long been masking as Baby Dolls in short sexy dresses. Black New Orleans culture liberally supported cross-dressing for men and women. Both during the Carnival season and on Mardi Gras Day and in the club scene, the fluidity of gender identities and sexual desire was in play. In the club scene, popular transvestite performers at the Dew Drop Inn, the famous musicians' haunt at 2836 LaSalle Street, were reigned over by Irving Ale, whose stage name was "Patsy Vidalia." Ale had been influenced by trans performers at the Black nightclub Caledonia around the late 1930s. It was in this fertile soil that "Little Richard" Penniman's alter ego, "Princess Lavonne," would be planted a decade later.[18] In more sacred and less profane spaces, Leafy Anderson, founder of the Black Spiritual church movement in New Orleans, hired jazz bands for social and religious purposes. Anderson also cross-dressed during religious plays that she arranged and starred in at her church.

Kenneth Leslie grew up in the Calliope Project[19] in uptown New Orleans. This Third Ward neighborhood bordered the streets of Dorgenois, Roman, Martin Luther King Drive (formerly Melpomene), and Iroquois. When Leslie was ten (around 1961),[20] he overheard his mother and her friends debating a heated issue concerning the politics of the Baby Doll maskers in their neighborhood. Elizabeth Russell, Janice Smith, and his mother, Clothilde Kennedy Leslie, were discussing the intrigue surrounding a new group of Baby Dolls and a controversial encounter on Rampart

Street: "The older/original Baby Dolls thought these new Baby Dolls were prissy and not really representative of what the Baby Doll culture was all about. They understood the Baby Doll culture-of-old" as "a rougher group of women" who "got together to do what baby dolls did. A new group of women were more of what we think a lady would be like. Baby Dolls of old had a different way of carrying themselves. I knew nothing of the claims of prostitution, but maybe that is what my mother was talking about."

The Baby Dolls were angry that another group of women was masking and that these new women were not seen as streetwise, or true to the older women's image of what the masking tradition was all about. In their view, these interlopers were taking over the image they had so carefully constructed over the years, and "the older generation did not care for that. They were willing to fight or they had fought. Whatever went down, it did so on Rampart Street." Ms. Leslie and her friends "knew what the Baby Dolls were about and they weren't surprised that if someone came in to try to take their culture, . . . the Baby Dolls would have an uprising against them."

PERFORMING FEMININITY: MALE BABY DOLLS TRANSGRESSING GENDER ROLES

Some of the women didn't look so good and some looked like men.
—Kenneth Leslie, born 1951

Baby Doll groups included a few men who would parade dressed either in satin shirts and pants, in costumes such as police officers, or in the Baby Doll costumes. There may have been some gay men who paraded together as Baby Dolls. In addition, the Batiste family's custom of parading as the "Dirty Dozen" band included throngs of young Black men who would borrow their female relatives' clothes to mask as women. The band extended its cross-dressing tradition to playing local performances. Their attention-getting attire, combined with their musical strength, catapulted them to notoriety.[21]

Royce Osborn's documentary *All on a Mardi Gras Day* contains one of the few detailed examples of African American men's penchant for masking elegantly as women. On Carnival before integration, a great deal of male and female cross-dressing is said to have taken place. But the paucity of research on the subject requires stretching a bit to the musical

"Street scene during Carnival of African Americans in costume in New Orleans, Louisiana, in the 1930s." From the Collection of the U.S. Works Progress Administration of Louisiana, courtesy State Library of Louisiana.

world, where there is documented evidence of the "female impersonator" tradition at the legendary Dew Drop Inn. In 2011, Millisia White and I asked Tremé musician Lionel Batiste to try to identify or give context to the cross-dressed African American men in images from the 1930s and 1940s captured by WPA photographers. While he did not recognize them as Baby Dolls, the photos do provide evidence of the popularity of African American male cross-dressing, gender-bending, and transgressive homosociality.

Robert McKinney reported on the incident that probably led to the decline of Baby Doll masking on St. Joseph's feast night. Recalling March 19, 1940, McKinney titled his essay, "Captain Jackson Keeps the Baby Dolls from Strutting Their Stuff." He described the nature of the event in detail:

> St. Joseph night was clear, slightly chilly, but perfectly swell for mirth, especially Baby Doll fun. This is the night that is usually a second Mardi Gras for a lot of people, i.e., Baby Dolls and their ilk. They mask and wave their hips, sing low down blues songs to the accompaniment of loud cornets, banjos, drums and other instruments. They frolic on the streets much in the same manner as they do on Fat Tuesday; their shimmies are strictly solid and always attract large crowds.
>
> In their minds, they had built up St. Joseph night as "the biggest

African American male maskers, photo taken by Joseph O. Misshore. From the *Louisiana Weekly* Photograph Collection, Amistad Research Center, Tulane University.

night we ever had"; they had re-pressed their long-waisted, pleated skirts of bright colors and had turned enough tricks to have green backs in their stockings. Nothing was going to stop the Baby Dolls, not even a storm. "There is always an inside."

Well, there was no storm, but something happened that was much worse, its effects are still being felt and promulgated. The Archbishop stepped into the picture and said there should not be any masking because it fell in the Lenten Season. He suggested April 2 instead. Like Jennie Watts said, "Who is the Archbishop? He ain't none of our pappy," and she is a Baby Doll whose attitudes about most things is definitely indifferent. Because the Archbishop made himself clear in the matter, Captain Jackson of the First Precinct sent out a word that there must be no masking, only a few Baby Dolls accepted his message; they promised to mask and were going to do so. They were so persistent the usually calm police captain became irate and contacted them himself. Baby Irene, some kind of dictator in Baby Doll affairs, stated, "The Captain says, 'I don't want no masking, and if any of you do, so I'm going put your black asses in jail.' Cause, I personally wouldn't give a fuck, but I don't feel like going back to jail. I just got out."

. . . There were only three masked Baby Dolls present: their rusty legs peeped from under short, satin skirts which were tight around their posteriors. Masking was very light among some of the Baby Dolls for the first time in twenty years. One of the more peppery Baby Dolls said she didn't give a damn what the Archbishop said, she was going to mask, and she did so. This dishpan-faced Baby Doll must have been charged with a "weed" cigarette (she was certainly "togged" down in a short red skirt with a cowboy-like hat) because she left the scene literally walking on air, stating, "I'm going to the Tick Tock and I'm high as a kite." Somebody chided, "You ain't never get in no Tick Tock, that's high class nigger winch." The "chick" laughed, but changed her mind about going to the Tick Tock.

According to *Cassell's Dictionary of Slang,* in the nineteenth century "chick" was slang for a man. In the 1940s "chick" could refer to a male prostitute. It was only in the mid-twentieth century, from the 1950s onward, that "chick came to represent a term for women and the things women would be interested in, such as [a] 'chick movie.'"[22] The quotation marks around the word "chick" in McKinney's typed transcript is evidence that the Baby Doll in question was probably a man.

Documented evidence of Black men in New Orleans doing drag or masking as women dates back to the 1920s. Marybeth Hamilton noted that the Black female-impersonation performative genre that emerged from Black working-class culture was widely appealing to all strata of African Americans and to interracial couples.[23] Both were groups who attended the frequent and annual drag balls and galas from the 1920s through the 1950s. Their events also garnered the devoted attention of the Black press. It is almost unimaginable today to picture the Black press according significant cultural weight and fawning on Black gay culture, yet prior to integration, this indeed was their posture. Thaddeus Russell writes that

both *Ebony,* which began publishing in 1945, and *Jet,* founded in 1951, gave regular, prominent, and positive coverage of the drag balls in Chicago, New York, and Detroit, and through the early 1950s regularly featured articles on homosexuality. *Jet* claimed that drag balls were staged in "nearly every big U.S. Negro community." The typical article on the balls in the magazines passed no negative judgments, and included several photos of drag queens dancing with and kissing men, as well as detailed descriptions of the performers' outfits. The "female impersonators" were "dazzling," "stunning," "vivacious," and "more shapely than [a] burlesque queen."[24]

Black female impersonators were an exciting mainstay attraction for 1940s audiences that gathered at local bars and jazz clubs in New Orleans. Barred from White establishments, Blacks were not about to forgo the entertainments of the adult pleasure industries. Clubs like the Dew Drop Inn, Caledonia, the Club Desire, and the Club Tijuana regularly booked gender-bending acts. The most famous of these was the aforementioned Patsy Vidalia, born Irving Ale in 1921 in Vacherie, Louisiana. Patsy fancied herself as the "Toast of New Orleans," and sponsored an annual gala that was considered an important social event.

THE PROCESSION: A RITUAL JOURNEY ON CARNIVAL DAY

Over time, the African American community developed a style of communication about its claims to self-definition through ritualized processions along public streets. Writer and cultural historian Kalamu ya Salaam describes these journeys as part of an aesthetic: "Unlike the Eurocentric tradition of a centralized place (museums, galleries, exhibitions, etc.) which the people go to in order to view the best artwork, the African tradition emphasizes literally moving the art through the community. Again, the tradition is 'masked' as a Mardi Gras parade which is both acceptable to the dominant society and within the means of the Black community."[25] In the early days of the Zulu parade, routes were not predictable but always included stops for varying lengths of time at spots in which there were either business relationships or historic significance to the paraders.

The Mardi Gras Indians are legendary for their lack of predictability. Writing from an anthropological perspective, Kathryn VanSpanckeren has interpreted the processions of the Mardi Gras Indians as an archetypal journey of the hero who prepares to meet, confront, and overcome a challenge and then return to the community stronger, wiser, and with a greater ability to solidify the unity of the group: "The tribe's wandering journey like the parade is a quest involving going forth to battle and returning victorious. Its route is unpredictable."[26] What's more, the "call, setting forth, confrontation, combat, and return in triumph—song cycles embody a communal vision in which the hero wins a boon, not for himself, but for the entire community he embodies."[27] Chants proclaiming one's greatness, dance movements meant to embody prowess, and challenges of daring and insults in the tradition of heroic boasting prior to undertaking epic battles are part of the processional script for many African American street-masking and parading traditions.

Community members over the years established a tradition of forming support groups in which tragedies and triumphs could be shared. They called these small collectives social aid and pleasure clubs. Some of these celebrate their communion through annual second-line parades. Helen Regis has characterized these gatherings as public processions that "transform urban space, creating an alternative social order that private clubs actualize by 'taking it to the streets' in those very neighborhoods ordinarily dominated by the quotidian order of inner-city poverty and spatial apartheid."[28] These processions often consist of club members, a brass band, and thousands of supporters expressing the experiences and collective concerns of the group in their sociopolitical and aesthetic reality. They do so following the script that seems common to African American material-culture practices. The ritual play of the second line consists of "fierceness and clowning, respectability and signifying, freedom and the memory of slavery." All of these "figure into the discussion of parade performance."[29]

Mercedes Stevenson, who masked as a Baby Doll with two of her close friends in the early 1970s, and who is the current Big Queen of the Wild Tchoupitoulas Mardi Gras Indians, provides a window into the world of the impromptu processions that were part of children's lives in her Twelfth Ward neighborhood.[30] The children in the neighborhood would form a line behind a young man some years their senior. He led them downtown, a journey of a good distance from their homes. Most of the time he sang "Tone the Bell": "We would be dancing and hollering like him. People would be looking at us. We would go all the way down town to St. Bernard Avenue. He would have all of us behind. We would be dancing down. He did that for years." Toning the bell was part of African American Protestant culture. Church bells had differing tones depending on what message was being sent out. But to tone the bell was to send out a particular communication. The song "Tone the Bell" has the refrain "so glad, done got over, done got over at last." It speaks on multiple levels of the hardships encountered in this world and how, through baptism, faith, and ultimately death, the singer makes it to heaven to speak with Jesus and God to tell of all the troubles that life on earth imposed.

Stevenson "grew up with the second line." A neighbor, Arthur "Pawran" Dillon, known for his dapper dress and his philanthropy, would hire two members of the Olympia Brass Band just so the children could dance and parade. Perhaps his devotion to the children was an extension of his community commitment as a member of social and pleasure groups, notably the Young Men Olympians, a benevolent association, and the Prince of Wales, a pleasure club. Stevenson remembered the formal second-line parades of the social and pleasure clubs with affection and a sense of agency:

We would just get together and start parading. We started from the 12th ward and we would march down to where a lot of bars were in the neighborhood. Musicians went around in a truck and they would get out and play and dance. We would follow them on foot. We knew where they were going. At that time the Prince of Wales Club which started about 1923 would follow the parade. Some members would dress like policemen and ride on horses. A man named Samuel would hire a carriage and ride in it and be a captain. It would be all Black people. It was a lot of fun because it was the people who knew people. They did not have much, but what they had they use to share. It was a fun thing for Black people because they always knew music and they always loved music. It was the thing that kept them going during segregation. It was what the Blacks had for themselves and now it has grown bigger and bigger. It is beginning to be recognized.

Stevenson was able to witness the uptown Baby Dolls, who were women of her community and respected ones at that:

When I was coming up I use to watch Geneva Tapps, Martha Tapps, and Mozella [last name unknown]. They would be so much fun.[31] They would be in those short dresses. They had bloomers underneath and they would pull their dresses up. We would follow them to the White bar room. The owner would open up the doors to them because it was Carnival. They would be dancing and be all on the counter. They would wear short dresses, baby doll hats, ruffles, stockings to the thigh. They had garters on the stockings pulled to the knee and bloomers. It was satin, pink, blue, and yellow. When we masked in the 1970s, I made our costumes something like that but we wore socks and we had ballerina shoes.

When they weren't masking on Carnival, I know they did housework. At that time folks did not have too many good jobs just working for White people in their houses, cooking, taking care of their children and doing their laundry.

They were good time women. They liked the good times. They drank. They use to make their own wine—let the grapes age and—when it was bootleg they made their own liquor. They played cards and had fish fries. They charged twenty-five cents for fish, potato salad, bread, and macaroni. Sometime they would make either file gumbo or okra gumbo. They played the gramophone and you would think you were in a joint somewhere. They would cut up. They'd have the house rocking. They knew how to party and how to enjoy themselves. They were popular women. People liked them. Those three were always together. They died around the 1970s.

In the 1970s, Stevenson and her friends Caroline and Eloise decided to mask.

The first year we dressed in pants. We decided we weren't going to do this next year. We decided to dress as Baby Dolls. Caroline's color was pink and Eloise's was green. My color was gold. I did all the sewing. Carol asked, "What are we going to do with our shoes?" We got a clear material like a table cloth and we fixed them up. We made the bonnets from like a long time ago. We got a pinafore and put the bow in the back. The dresses were short. We had socks on like the babies. Everybody would say, "Oh here come the Baby Dolls." People were taking pictures and Caroline use to pull her dress up. My daughter Mary Kim was eight and her friends thought we were cute. While we were walking around, we danced. We cherished that dancing.

After three years, George Landry (or Chief Jolly), the man who started the Wild Tchoupitoulas and who had been masking alone, asked Mercedes, Caroline, and Eloise to come and mask with him.

He said, "ya'll mask every year, why don't ya'll mask and come with us." Carol said she always wanted to be an Indian anyway. We got together and got the colors together. Caroline and Eloise masked until 1977. I stayed with them in 1987 with Charles Taylor from the 7th ward. Now most of my family is Wild Tchoupitoulas Mardi Gras Indians.

THE GOLDEN SLIPPER BABY DOLLS AND THEIR LEGACY

Walter and Alma Trepagnier Batiste had a large family. As parents they used art, culture, and masking to keep their children—Miriam, Norman, Lionel, Walter, Rodney, Ferdinand, Henry, Arthur, Alma, Elvidge, and Felicia— engaged and under their watchful eye. Alma formed the Golden Slipper Club,[32] a group of women and men that masked as Baby Dolls and as the Dirty Dozen. These Baby Dolls followed the ritual pattern of the African American community, parading in their neighborhood, singing Creole and ribald songs, and stopping for refreshments at maskers' homes to the delight of the children who waited in anticipation for them to arrive. As she aged and became more devoted to her spiritual life, Alma stopped masking. After her parents died, as did those who had masked with them, Miriam felt a void. In the late 1970s, Miriam decided to mask. She gathered together her sister, Felicia, her brothers, nieces, and nephews to bring back their family tradition. The news spread like wildfire, and as many as eighteen women joined her and her family.

Jerry Brock, the co-founder of New Orleans radio station WWOZ, had the opportunity to witness the revival of the Batiste family tradition.

We met at 7 AM at Felicia Shezbie's house on Orleans Avenue. A huge breakfast with eggs, pork chops, gumbo, biscuits, gravy, greens, rice and desserts was the morning meal.

Following breakfast Precisely Batiste led a prayer for our safety and to have a beautiful day. Then we hit the streets.

We paraded from 8 AM Fat Tuesday until 2 AM the following morning. There was a loosely organized route with rest periods. We strutted through huge crowds on Claiborne with ease and grace. They played old ribald songs, jazz tunes and Creole songs. Everyone loved the Baby Dolls and thousands of revelers cleared a path for the Baby Dolls and the Dirty Dozen.

In the middle of a gigantic crowd, a space would magically open and there would be a three-legged card table barely standing with a fifth of Jack Daniels for the Baby Dolls and Dozen. It was more surreal than a Fellini film. The next stop might be gumbo and sandwiches.

A lesser-known but striking group of Baby Dolls from further downtown were known as Satan (spelled Satin) and Sinners. Film footage shows Satan with his red union drawers and with white cotton boxers worn outside. Along with his long red tail and his red horns he carried a decorated umbrella. A man carried a sign saying "Satin and Sinners" and the Baby Dolls followed three abreast strutting in red satin baby doll outfits.

Others have claimed that the Baby Dolls were just prostitutes who masked on Mardi Gras. But that seriously oversimplifies it. They were hard working people caught up in the life they were dealt but made the most of. They stuck together and created an ironic twist unlike any other.

These people, born into a repressed condition, turned it around and made a brilliant creation of live art. The joy they spread changed the path of culture worldwide. The Baby Dolls were a welcome and unique part of an African-American renaissance centered in New Orleans.[33]

THEY CALL ME BABY DOLL

A note on the use of monikers is in order. Danny Barker described the process by which children were given nicknames that followed them literally from the cradle to the grave. The "pet names" were based on how a mother felt about her child. These were generally flattering terms of endearment. Older people, he asserted, were not so generous.

"Let me see him." Then they pin a nickname on you. "That's little Egg Head." "Why you call my child Egg Head?" "He got a Egg Head." "That's little Cokey." "Why you call my child little Coke?" "Because he's got a coconut head." They pin a nickname on you right. . . . If you look in obituaries of the *New Orleans Times Picayune* you will see, when they list all the people that have passed away, they always put that nickname there, because some people in your life never knew your real name. They knew you by your nickname.[34]

The practice of naming individuals with additional referents over and above the given name extended to the jazz world. In his article "The Slang of Jazz,"[35] H. Brook Webb noted that almost all jazz musicians had nicknames. Not only that, the instruments had nicknames, and a whole vocabulary emerged that described the style of playing of the musician, the style of the band, and the reaction of the audience to the music, including dances such as "truckin'" and the Lindy or the Hop. The name of the dance "truckin'" emerged from men who worked as railroad porters. The truck was their main tool to carry the luggage of the passengers. When they were weary, they would say that they were going to "truck on home."

The moniker of the Baby Doll likewise emerged in a sense from the occupation of the women maskers. One can almost image Clara Belle Moore saying with a swagger, "Sure, they call me Baby Doll, that's my name. They have been calling me Baby Doll for a long time."[36] Many generations of Baby Dolls had monikers representing their public identities. Miriam Batiste Reed could not recall many of the given names of the women and men who masked with her mother because they all were referred to by their nicknames. "Mama Goo," for instance, was the moniker for Alma Borden, a member of Alma Batiste's Golden Slipper Baby Dolls, according to Reed.

BABY DOLLS AND BEYOND

Those who masked as Baby Dolls rarely did so for a lifetime. It seemed that Baby Doll masking was part of a long career of cultural and ritual participation. Maskers went on to become Mardi Gras Indians, ordained ministers in Spiritual churches, or grand marshals for social and pleasure clubs.

Mardi Gras Indians

Allison "Tootie" Montana, the late Big Chief of the Yellow Pocahontas tribe, was regarded as the Big Chief of all the Mardi Gras Indian gangs regardless of the ward they represented. He was an expert on all the African American masking traditions, having participated in several and having watched the evolution of most. In his words:

I've been making masks for more than forty years. I know how to make all the outfits. I can make the skeleton outfit, the baby doll outfit (with black shirts, pink blouses with puffed sleeves, black mask, a black whip, black boots). The men with the Baby Dolls would take two pairs of shoes and make one out of them so they'd be twice as long. I masked with the Baby Dolls about twice, and then I masked with the skeleton about three times before I masked Indian.

During my early years they had the Rosebud Social and Pleasure Club—women who use to mask. Even all the gay people use to mask. They dressed in women's clothes, expensive lace and stockings. Men use to mask as women, and there were even women who would mask as men. The masks were made out of screen wire. The Million Dollar Babies were women who had money, ten, twenty, and fifty dollar bills in their stockings.[37]

The Spiritual Church

Miriam Batiste Reed recalled that her mother, Alma, became an ordained minister in the Spiritual church "after she finished masking," and in effect, so did the entire family. As Reed noted, "that turned us on to singing and we went to a lot of churches." Louis and Fannie Reimonenq masked in the satin dresses of the Baby Doll with the Golden Slipper Social and Pleasure Club, led by Alma Batiste. And for this couple, too, spirituality transitioned them from Carnival maskers to leaders of sacred rites.

Arnold Louis Reimonenq was born on October 9, 1894, to Jules Reimonenq and Mary Hoel. He was the eldest of seventeen children. After Mary died in 1899, Jules married Lucille (Lucy) Coulon. In the 1910 census, Jules listed his father as French and his mother as being from Louisiana. The couple's race was reported as mulatto. Jules was a carpenter based out of his home, and Lucy did not list an occupation. Louis married Fannie Buckingham in 1917. According to the 1930 census, they lived at 914 North Robertson. They had an adopted son, Rudolph Cressy (age seven) and boarded a lodger, Richard Smith (age thirty-two). Fannie was not listed as working outside the home. Elaine Gutierrez, Louis's niece, described her Uncle "Louie" as the patriarch of the family. Everyone turned to him for help with their problems. He was concerned about the family's welfare from birth to death. He belonged to many organizations and was a leader within the Freemasons, a secret society. Yet, he was also "happy go lucky," outgoing, and liked to have fun. Like Alma Batiste, Louis and Fannie became increasingly involved in their spiritual lives as they aged.

About 1942, Louis founded Calvary Spiritual Church on St. Philip and Liberty streets in New Orleans, now a historic landmark. When Fannie died on November 4, 1951, a wake was held for two nights at the Emile Labat Funeral Home, and she was given the rites of the Eastern Star. Even though Louis was the leader of the Calvary Spiritual Church, the final service took place at St. Augustine Catholic Church. Louis died on August 26, 1967. His third wife, Florence Reimonenq, continued the leadership of Calvary Spiritual Church. Florence was featured in a 1969 *Ebony* article, "Black Astrologers Predict the Future."[38] She died in 1989.

Grand Marshal

Although the Gold Digger Baby Doll tradition allows Lois Nelson a freedom of expression that borders on ribaldry, when she comes out as the grand marshal over many jazz events, her presentation is solemn. There are two different kinds of grand marshals: one for a jazz funeral and one for a social aid and pleasure club. Merline Kimble noted that she has never seen Lois do the kinds of things she does as a Baby Doll when she is a grand marshal. The grand marshal of the social aid and pleasure club parades on the street in colorful clothes and accessories. Participants form a second line and "dance, march, monkey shine, and do it all. As a grand marshal for a jazz funeral the attire is black and white. The movements are regulated. You have to be in an army type step. You do the dirge. You have to know how to dismiss that body. To let that hearse pass when that body is passing; there is a certain way you have to put your hand behind your back. You do that one two, that kind of step."[39]

● ● ● ● ● ● ● ● ● ● ● ● **5** ● ● ● ● ● ● ● ● ● ● ● ●

"We Are No Generation"

Resurrecting the Central Role of Dance to the Creation of New Orleans Music

We are no generation. We represent our ancestors; those that danced before us.
—*Davieione (Beauty from the East) Fairley, New Orleans
Society of Dance's Baby Doll Ladies*

● ●

I N 1940 ROBERT MCKINNEY asked, "Who is this Baby Doll and why is she referred to as such?" The answer lies in the co-location of the sociopolitical world in which these women were embedded with vernacular cultural traditions. By 1912, New Orleans Black expressive culture was taking on an enduring form of musicality to shape and influence the century's artistry and popular culture. Buddy Bolden, a major originator of the "hot" jazz style, innovatively blended blues, marches, and Black spirituals in a manner that appealed to New Orleans's Black youth. The Million Dollar Baby Dolls were also part of a new "youth culture," one that would increasingly and self-consciously come to see itself as rebelling against mainstream culture and society.

As poor women, the original Baby Dolls worked in the District, some as shift workers, and returned to their homes in Black working-class neighborhoods outside the District after their workday, unlike others who were absorbed by the underworld activities of gambling and petty crime in addition to prostitution.[1] There was a permeable boundary between the District and middle-class life that some women used to good effect. These multiply identified women were part of the nighttime performative landscape that included dancing, singing, playing as musicians on a par with men in jazz bands, and participating in the religious traditions of the Black Spiritual church, Catholicism, and Voodoun. For example, Eddie Dawson remembered a woman in the 1910s from Back o' Town who played jazz at night and organ at St. Katherine's Church during the day. Neliska "Baby" Briscoe's mother, Neliska Thomas Mitchell, worked at St. Ann's Church caring for the priests and nuns of the parish by day and at night took her eight- or nine-year-old daughter to perform as a dancer and singer at Alley Cabaret. They were Black women in a White-supremacist and male-dominated society. The ability to earn a decent leaving and be respected by their peers was challenged by the limitations of their employment and educational opportunities and the exclusion of women's participation in political affairs that determined the very laws by which they were governed in the District and in society as a whole. Yet they managed to have an undiminished sense of their own self-worth.

There are several enduring themes of the Baby Doll phenomenon. The first is the relationship between the women's dances and the music of the times. The second is the women's reappropriation of feminine symbols to critique and satirize the limitations on their sex, imposed by patriarchal legal and social norms. Third is the women's own view of themselves as "tough," resilient trendsetters and unconventional community leaders. Finally, as "women dancing the jazz" (from jass/jazz to swing, to bebop, to rhythm and blues, to hip hop and bounce), they carry a message of hope and resilience to a community that has always relied on its culture to make it through life.

MUSIC AND DANCE

When Robert McKinney interviewed Beatrice Hill in 1940, she had lost much of her money and was living in the most deplorable of rooming houses populated by drug users and petty criminals. He described her unflatteringly as a dope fiend and syphilitic patient at Charity Hospital. Seemingly immune to the harsh condemnations of those outside her ranks, she evidenced no lack of enthusiasm in recounting her heyday working in the District. Even before they masked as Baby Dolls one Mardi Gras Day, women such as Beatrice inhabited a world whose center was ironically at the intersection of the streets called Liberty and Gravier. There, one might say, they met their restricted freedoms with much grit. McKinney made the wry observation that their attitudes were indifferent, their profanity that of a sailor, and they were prideful.

They wore short dresses, danced with money in their stockings, and sang erotically charged blues songs. And they danced. At work, they danced nude and on the tops of tables and bar counters. They competed to see who could "shimmy" the best. They would lie on the floor while men fed them candy. As dark-skinned Black women, they were barred from places that catered exclusively to White men, like Lulu White's brothel, Mahogany Hall, for purposes of either work or their own entertainment. Instead, they frequented bars like the Elite and the Black and Tan. The Silver Platter was especially popular when they got off work. It was the after-hours gathering spot for musicians. They dressed up and carried their own money as a show of pride and independence. If they were working downtown, they referred to the women uptown as "rats." If they were uptown women, they saw the downtown women's attitude of superiority as thinking their "asses were silver." Their rivalries extended to jealousy over men, money, and their frocks. They fought each other with "boiling" words and hair pulling. Robert Tallant recorded that "crashing the gate" was a common practice of rival groups of prostitutes, "white, black, brown, yellow and pink." One group arrived uninvited to the ball of another and forced their way in. There was usually a melee culminating in police intervention.[2]

It was out of this rivalry among similarly positioned women that a masking tradition was born. "All we wanted to do was to show them up," Hill told McKinney. First, Hill's gang, with the aid of a local police officer, invaded a party that was being given exclusively by and for downtown women and their circle. Beatrice and her gang did not simply attend, they entered and took over. They staged a "show" in which Julia Ford got on top of a table, proceeding to "shake on down," and then the other dancers disrobed her. In the tradition of the cutting contests, Beatrice had wanted the band to play "Shake that Thing" and dedicate it to her. A brawl ensued, and several people went to jail. But Beatrice had made her point as a rumor developed that her group had a million dollars in cash on them. Armed with their dance routines, their short sexy attire, their bodacious attitudes, and a street-carnival culture that empowered them to participate in the public rituals of their community, all these women needed was a name. The brawl gave them that and the notoriety that they desperately sought. They took this panache and turned it into a legacy.

Inasmuch as the business of the District controlled the nature of the economic fortunes of Black women who were among its laborers, the sex industry itself formed and shaped the worldviews of the men, both Black and White, who produced and consumed it. Unconfined to the District, men took that view back to their homes and professional lives. That worldview specifically connoted how the arrangement between the sexes would be instigated, propagated, and integrated into everyday hierarchical arrangements that put women in general, but Black women in particular, squarely at the bottom of the social ladder. To dance for money was one employment "opportunity" available to uneducated poor Black women that existed among a small array of similarly poorly situated jobs: domestic or agricultural worker. The Million Dollar Baby Dolls danced for money. They danced for cultural purposes of participating in the life of the community through the second-line parades. They danced as well to demonstrate just how empowered they felt inside their spirits.

The primary purpose for which musicians played jazz was to provide music for dancers.[3] By the end of the first decade of the twentieth century, African American dance halls in New Orleans were showcasing bands that, rather than relying on sheet music, were improvising their songs. The dances that accompanied this new energetic music were seen as sensual.[4] Dances such as the shimmy or the shake and the Lindy Hop grew up from African American vernacular dance's interplay with jazz music.[5] Though the majority of African American musicians during this time were primarily concerned with playing songs for dancers, jazz is hardly remembered today as dance music.

The shift in jazz from dance music to music for concert-hall appreciation, along with the widening appeal of the jam session beyond the musicians themselves, began slowly in the 1930s and was firmly established by the late 1940s due to sweeping social changes. First, there was the migration of Black musicians from the South to the North and the attraction of young White audiences to this new genre. They too danced to the music, but they also would surround the stage to listen to the improvising musician whose creative genius was being evaluated and appreciated. A second change came with World War II, when people had more money, due to war-related industry, but fewer opportunities to travel as gasoline was in short supply. New options arose for delivering adult entertainment. Entrepreneurs began booking otherwise empty concert halls, auditoriums, and even movie theaters in local neighborhoods and began to include jazz bands along with a variety of other entertainment. A third factor was the venue itself. The stateliness of the concert halls seemed to demand something more from the audiences, the musicians, and the producers of these events. Prominent musicians like Duke Ellington began writing multi-movement compositions. Musicians and music critics alike seemed to trend toward creating distance in the relationship between jazz and popular entertainment. A fourth element concerned the decline of the dance band. The high wages that musicians had come to expect during the war made large dance bands unaffordable. Some, like Count Basie, returned to playing dance music and shifted their focus from the "looking" audience to the dancing one. Smaller bands emerged and fit the new "bebop" style that African American musicians such as Charlie Parker were inventing. Even though bebop would not completely sever its connection with dance, a new paradigm was in place, demanding that jazz's concert artists were to be accorded respect.[6]

When they mask, the Baby Dolls carry the unbroken relationship of jazz (including New Orleans's latest Black musical forms) to dance. In an article aptly titled "'Remember When?' Carnival on Claiborne Is Relived," Rhonda McKendall wrote:

> The Baby Dolls were something to see. Every year they flaunted a different get-up, but they always donned bloomers and tight skirts, 10 to 12 inches above the knee. Sometimes they wore false long curls topped with bonnets, derbies or pill box hats.
>
> Backed by a combo, the Dolls' steppin' out time was 10 AM sharp—rain, hail, sleet or what have you. And as the saying goes, "they would shake up a storm."
>
> They'd raise their walking canes or tambourines high in the air, rhythmically shaking their bodies to the ground.
>
> Not to be upstaged, the Gold Diggers would show up in elaborate apparel. They were more or less remembered for displaying money in their stockings and flirting with male spectators.
>
> When the Baby Dolls and Gold Diggers weren't stealing the show there were groups of second-liners, including men dressed like women, some making music with washtubs.[7]

On the streets on Carnival Day, during second-line parades at funerals, or on St. Joseph feast night, jazz and dance never lost their symbiotic

Gold Digger Baby Dolls at a Baby Doll celebration. The Dolls wear velvet and have walking canes. The men of the group wear top hats and satin shirts and pants; one is dressed as a policeman. From the Collection of the U.S. Works Progress Administration of Louisiana, courtesy State Library of Louisiana.

"Baby Doll celebration at Pete's Blue Heaven. The music box and tambourines are providing the music." 1942. Pete's Blue Heaven Lounge, one of the preeminent jazz clubs of its time, was located at 449 South Rampart Street. According to a jazz history walking-tour brochure from the National Park Service, it was "often both a starting and ending place for Zulu Social Aid and Pleasure Club funerals." From the Collection of the U.S. Works Progress Administration of Louisiana, courtesy State Library of Louisiana.

relationship. Somewhere, some women in the community would continue the relationship between dance and music.

In a Mardi Gras song popular among Creole-speaking Black New Orleanians called "That Is the Gossip, Shut Up!" a woman discovers her man is two-timing her and she vows to leave him. There was fluidity in the way the singer could start the song, but it was a duet. One singer announces what the gossip around town is about the woman, and the other singer laments. The accompanying dance is one in which the singers put their hands on their hips and gyrate to the tune.[8] The lyrics are as follows:

> That is the gossip, shut up!
> Aye-ya! I am going to quit,
> Me, I'm going to quit. I am going to quit.

The Mardi Gras Indians make music at a Baby Doll celebration. Written on photo: "Tambourine player beating out some 'Indian jive' for spectators." From the Collection of the U.S. Works Progress Administration of Louisiana, courtesy State Library of Louisiana.

> That is the gossip, shut up!
> Me don't like man has two women.
> Me lonesome girl, me don't like that.
> No, I'm going to quit my cheri.
> Me don't like a man has two women.
> That is the gossip, shut up!
> Aye-ya-ya! Me going to quit
> Me don't like that. Me going to quit.
> That is the gossip, shut up!

The Baby Doll masking tradition is a living legacy. As with the Mardi Gras Indians, the Skeletons, and the Zulu Social Aid and Pleasure Club, the number of people participating in the Baby Doll tradition has waxed and waned over the last century. (See appendix B for a list of known participants.)

Resa "Cinnamon Black" Wilson-Bazile (*second from left*) with Royce Osborn and other revelers, Mardi Gras 2011. Photograph by Reubin Phillip Colwart, used with permission.

Resa (Cinnamon Black) Wilson-Basile was introduced to the Baby Dolls as a teenager. As she recalls, "When I was fourteen, I saw these girls dancing and they looked like girls but they were women. They were so cute and they were having so much fun. They had all this money in their stockings. My grandmother wouldn't let me watch them. There was another group and she would let me watch them. They weren't dressed as solicitously as the other girls in the red stain dresses. These women had baby doll little panties that came down to their knees, and nice pretty laces. They had a good time. They hung out with the jazz band and you know when the jazz band comes out, everybody comes out."[9]

As an eyewitness to the bifurcated nature of the Baby Doll tradition, Cinnamon Black contrasts groups of maskers for whom expressing raw sexuality and transgressing norms for women was an end in itself with groups of maskers for whom portraying a Baby Doll became loaded with other meanings.[10] In fact, people masked as Baby Dolls for a variety of reasons. One woman I interviewed said that because she grew up poor, she never had a doll of her own. To her, the ability to mask offered the opportunity to embody the very thing that was absent in her childhood. She became that which had been denied. Miriam Reed Batiste said, "As for me, I didn't have

Antoinette K-Doe (*center*) and Eva Perry (*right*), Mardi Gras Day, 2007, with unidentified reveler on St. Claude in the Tremé, between the Backstreet Cultural Museum and St. Augustine Church. Photograph by Reubin Phillip Colwart, used with permission.

a Baby Doll, because they wasn't making black baby dolls at that time. You had white baby dolls. I did not have a white baby doll." Her mother and neighbors became living dolls for their children. As Geannie Thomas put it, "When I was coming up, I always loved dolls and we were very poor. My mother had three girls. At Christmas we got candy, but never a doll."

Businesswomen had different motivations; the Baby Doll character costume became a marketing device. Antoinette K-Doe, Geannie Thomas, and Tee-Eva exemplify this theme. K-Doe thought that, through rekindling the practice, she would be able to keep her famous husband's name before the public and hence generate business for her lounge. Millisia White considers her masking within the realm of cultural ambassadorship, carrying on the tradition and extending it to stage shows and videography.

Cinnamon Black explains the varying styles of dance performed in the Baby Doll tradition:

Baby Doll dance movements change depending on the situation. The Baby Dolls came out at certain times: for funerals processions, on Mardi Gras, for parties, with jazz bands, on St. Joseph's night and for charity events. If Baby Dolls were going to visit senior citizens, they would do monkeyshine. That makes them happy. But when Baby Dolls get the seniors up to dance they should do a low-style dirge. With children, Baby Dolls just do second line and not impose on them something they were not supposed to see. At parades, Baby Dolls do everything. They are with their families and peers and it is a really good time.

If Baby Dolls are at a funeral they don't want to do movements that are going to hop into the air. Baby Dolls won't have their umbrellas open if they are presiding over a funeral. They dance to a dirge, and the movements are second line. Their feet are moving in the ground because someone is being buried. The dance has to express the feeling of the moment. Once the person goes inside the cemetery, and they are buried, St. Expedite is passed, and that is where the bones and skeletons reside; then the dance movements celebrate their life. You open your umbrella; let your hair down. Life is good to you. You are there for the deceased and the family. You want their family to have the strength to carry on. The closer you get to where the deceased grew up and lived and certain landmarks, you go from the dirge to the second line to the monkeyshine.

The Baby Doll dances are more alluring in some cases than second-line dance. You have to be eighteen years old or old enough to go inside the clubs. It is fun. Most of the women they had their own businesses and their husbands had their own businesses. These were important women, and on Mardi Gras Day they were able to let their hair down and have a good time.[11]

African American dance can be considered an intergenerational art form. Dance researcher Katrina Hazzard-Gordon[12] writes that African American dances are re-vamped renderings of dances that have been created in prior generations, some as far back as the antebellum period and some that can be identified as having African origins. Hazzard-Gordon noted that African American vernacular social dance is more than an individual pastime and a way of having fun and remaining fit. It has served as a major identity marker for individuals who are members of a community, who have a certain neuromuscular competence, and who can also send a political message of resistance through the body's movements. African American dance is filled with personal, sociocultural, psychological, and political connotations. These elements have been retained among Baby Doll maskers.

WHY BABY DOLLS DANCE TODAY

In the late 1970s, when her mother and father passed and some of the ladies that used to mask with them also died, Miriam Batiste Reed got together with her family as the Baby Dolls and the Dirty Dozen Kazoo Band. When the news got out that they were going to mask as Baby Dolls, about eighteen ladies came to mask with them. The Batiste family would fortify themselves for the journey with food and prayer. They would go from house to house, and some of those were set up to receive and honor them with food and drinks: "We use to come through Claiborne Ave and it was nice. We were also invited in our Baby Doll masking to WWOZ radio. . . . I did the talking about the Baby Dolls, how it started and who my family was." Miriam Batiste Reed's connection to the early Tremé neighborhood Baby Doll tradition makes her a sought-after figure on all things Baby Doll. She has taught subsequent maskers the meaning, the costuming, the accessories, the style, and the flair of the tradition. Filmmaker Royce Osborn arranged and observed one such workshop led by Reed: "She showed them how to walk: 'You got to have a walk to you.' You got to shake it a little bit."[13]

In the 1980s, sixth-generation Tremé resident Merline Kimble gathered a group of friends to revive her grandparents' Gold Diggers Club to mask as Baby Dolls. In recent years, they have masked on Carnival at the Backstreet Cultural Museum in New Orleans, in March on "Super Sunday" with the Mardi Gras Indians, and in August with the "Satchmo Salute" second-line parade. In the view of the city's youngest Baby Doll, Deja Andrews, "Sometimes I like being a Baby Doll. I like it when I get paid. Some people say they don't want to dress up in costumes because it is not Halloween. I like dancing. I am not embarrassed when people are looking at us parading. I feel happy; like I am in my own world."[14]

In early 2000, Antoinette K-Doe garnered quite a bit of media coverage of her revival of the Baby Dolls. With the knowledge and assistance of Miriam Batiste Reed, K-Doe held a workshop at her Mother-in-Law Lounge, on North Claiborne Avenue. Reed taught the women how to make the satin Baby Doll outfits. Plagued by the image of the Baby Dolls as prostitutes, K-Doe went to great pains to distinguish her group of busi-

Geannie Thomas (*top right*) and Miriam Batiste Reed (*bottom right*) were among the pallbearers at the funeral of Lloyd Washington. Photograph by Angelo Coclanis, used with permission.

Antoinette K-Doe (*left front*) and Miriam Batiste Reed (*right*). Photograph by Angelo Coclanis, used with permission.

ness owners and professional women from that stereotype. According to Eva Perry—founding member, K-Doe friend, and owner of Tee-Eva's New Orleans Praline Shop—the way they mask "is clean." Perry hands out pralines as the Baby Dolls march. "I want to make someone happy and it is nice to give back to the community. Even some youngsters want to be a Baby Doll someday." Their aim is to have fun and act as a social aid and pleasure club. They were the pallbearers at the funeral of Lloyd Washington, the last living member of the Ink Spots vocal group.[15]

The charitable activities of Ernie K-Doe's Baby Dolls are well-known. Their benevolent efforts include contributions to the New Orleans Musicians Clinic, feeding the homeless alongside the Sheriff's Department on Thanksgiving, and countless appearances in nursing homes and other venues to promote the culture. At their core, they are entertainers. According to founding member Geannie Thomas, "When I met Antoinette, she got me into dancing, and the Mardi Gras thing and parades. Now, I am a rhythm-and-blues dancer."[16]

New Orleans Society of Dance founder Millisia White grew up in the Sixth Ward and always wanted to become a Baby Doll. Her founding of a dance company coincided with the ravages of the aftermath of Hurricane Katrina. White was in the city during the flooding and reported, "We felt like everything was in jeopardy when Katrina happened." Together with her brother, turntablist DJ Hektik, and her mentor, Eddie Edwards, they brainstormed over how to "connect the people." They turned to "what has been constant since 1719. We have always been surviving extreme devastation of life and property. We wanted to resurrect the things that unified us—what makes New Orleans." White noted that

wherever jazz went the dance went, but the dance is hardly mentioned and it is such an oversight. Baby Dolls always chanted. Chanting is just like Indian jive. I remember them with the tambourines, with a small band. They had homemade tambourines back then. They would always sing and dance, like church, like old time when they would second line. We have updated the traditional dance and music with bounce, New Orleans underground, or the New Orleans vernacular of hip hop. DJ Hektik laid tracks under our chants. When we perform, we incorporate the tambourine and the cowbell and upgrade it with bounce, and it is a way for us to introduce it to the new generation.[17]

The aim of Millisia White's Baby Doll Ladies is to "put dance on the same platform as the music."

> We put the music, song, and dance together to do that. In 2007 we presented a proposal to the city and were awarded a small sponsorship to do shorts and info reels. My brother, DJ Hektik, was able to get the celebrities to join in. The celebrities liked the idea of the cultural resurrection and did not want to let the culture die. We want to shine light on all things being resurrected that are positive about the place. Holding true to our customs and culture, we started where we stood. We put on a floor show, a production benefit, and the city came out. We thought about what we could contribute; what could we resurrect. By means of videography performances, we informed the world about what Creole culture is all about: the artistry of it. In that way *we served as that example of hope.* If someone starts a band, we want to collaborate. We aren't waiting. We are doing it with the means at our hands.[18]

Since the beginning of the jazz age, the music has changed to keep up with the changes in dance steps. So it is today. The Baby Doll Ladies incorporate bounce, a New Orleans expression of hip hop. Bounce uses call and response, Mardi Gras Indian chanting, and dance call-outs. Consistent with the "raddy" tradition, bounce dancing is very sexual.

A TOUGHNESS OF SPIRIT AND A JOY FOR LIFE

The interview Millisia White and I conducted with Merline Kimble, Lois Nelson, and Patricia McDonald on a Sunday afternoon in April 2010 transitioned from why the women masked and continued to breathe life into the Gold Digger tradition to how they had met life's setbacks with a determined and steely will that they believed should be taught to other women in similar circumstances.[19]

When Lois Nelson performs her role as grand marshal for a funeral parade, she has developed a practice of dancing on the casket. Lois specialized in getting on top of the casket during the second-line part of the funeral. "They always ask me when they are rolling the casket, how can I dance on it. There is a certain way I grip my feet, my shoe that keep me from sliding."

Merline Kimble (in Baby Doll costume) at the funeral of Collins "Coach" Lewis, Mardi Gras Indian costume artist, August 13, 2011. Other maskers pictured are Bruce Sunpie Barnes, chief of the Northside Skull and Bones Gang (*far right*), and Victor Harris of Fi Yi Yi (*fourth from left*). Photograph by Keith Weldon Medley, used with permission.

Gold Digger Baby Dolls at the Louis Satchmo Salute, an annual second-line parade in Armstrong's honor. Photograph by Eli Prytikin, used with permission.

Her motivation is to "do unto others" what she would like to have done for her. Nelson believes that this is the way the person wants to go and they way she wants to go. "Get on top of me, have fun, and then let me go." Nelson's teenage son, Darnell "D-Boy" Andrews, was murdered at the age of seventeen in 1995.[20] Anthropologist Helen Regis witnessed the moving funerary tribute to a young man gunned down in what has become an epidemic of the loss of Black male youth, part of the vagaries of late-twentieth-century capitalism: a destructive masculine code of conduct and drug activity that satisfies greed, but that is also used for the mitigation of despair. Nelson recalled that when she stood on D-Boy's coffin she "didn't want to feel the emotion of crying. God had given me a time to be with him while he was living. Through his death was my time to rejoice." Music is what got her through. Kimble recalled that Lois placed stereo speakers in front of her home and played an Anita Baker CD non-stop for a week. The community tolerated her public display of grief. Though she "drove the block crazy" with the repetition, no one complained.

Reflecting on that time and the lessons she has learned from it, Nelson believes that the young people are oblivious to the effect the culture of violence will have on the people they leave behind. "Some mothers take it so hard. Some take it as days go by. There is nothing we can do about it. We can't bring them back, but we can find closure. I don't remember anything bad; I just remember the good times. Some mamas just crack up. They shouldn't crack up. They should have something where the strong mamas can tell the weak mothers how to be strong. We are trying to tell children about other ways of solving problems and being successful in life besides petty comparisons about who has what and who looks better." She longed for the time when music in Tremé was created out of the everyday occurrences of musicians living and working in the neighborhood. The children would get absorbed into their artistry, but that time has passed. Patricia McDonald, who has masked with the Gold Diggers and is an integral part of the Tremé community, added that she too had lost a son and that her way of managing the grief was to take ownership, so to speak, of his body: "I carried him in here for nine months and I carried him out. I was the pallbearer. They said, 'You can't do that.' My mama said, 'that is your child. You want to carry him, carry him. No one can tell you what to do with him. If you are strong enough, you carry him.'"

For the new-generation Baby Dolls of the New Orleans Society of Dance, lessons were learned following dislocation and relocation in the

A Skeleton and a Baby Doll. Photograph by Jeffrey Dupuis, used courtesy Millisia White.

New Orleans Society of Dance's Baby Doll Ladies with D J Hektik at the Tremé Villa. Photograph by Virnado Woods, used courtesy of Millisia White.

wake of Hurricane Katrina. The hurricane and its aftermath became part of their lexicon of expression. Kenethia "Lady N.O. Cutie" Morgan sees their dance as

> part of what we do; we need that music to express who we are, not as an individual, but as a group. The Baby Dolls express ourselves through dance and have fun doing it. One of the songs we dance to is by Free Agents Brass Band called "Made it through that Water." We all experienced Katrina, and we were all so glad to be back home. "We made it through that water, that muddy muddy water." It was bad how they had us on that bridge. We want to show people how we live; why we did what we did. We almost lost our city. Some almost lost their minds living in and out of hotel rooms. We all survived and that is something the parade crowd can relate to. It is now cultural because we all experienced a tragedy and made it through.[21]

Similarly, Davieione (Beauty from the East) Fairley states that

> you forget about the bad stuff and separate yourself from it. When we are masking and dancing, it is not about the bad stuff. We release the tension through dancing. That is where we get our energy and our motivation. We express ourselves to each other and the world. If we can go out there like we don't have a care in the world and dance, we can rub off on someone else that is going through something. This is New Orleans where we speak to each other on the street. Imagine what we can do as a group when we are performing in front of thousands. We are like them. It is just that we are together and we say, "It's OK to feel free."[22]

So what, then, is the answer to the question, "Who is this Baby Doll, and why is she referred to as such?" Baby Dolls are people full of fun who invite the community to be at play as a vital cultural reaffirmation of their faith in their own abilities to soldier on and meet life's unexpected challenges.

ACKNOWLEDGMENTS

N O WORK, carried out in love, is performed in isolation. I thank Millisia White, founder and director of the New Orleans Society of Dance, for an amazing experience in collaborative knowledge creation. Millisia and I met in January 2010 when she was sponsoring a fundraiser for the New Orleans Society of Dance's Baby Doll Ladies. After we discussed the lack of research on the Baby Doll masking tradition, she was open to my suggestion of interviewing Baby Doll maskers for an article. I contacted David Johnson, editor of *Louisiana Cultural Vistas* magazine, to see if there might be interest in publishing an article about the Baby Dolls. Millisia and I interviewed numerous participants in April 2010. After I drafted an article, Millisia shared what I had written with those interviewed. This feedback was incorporated, and the article was published in the Fall/Winter edition of *Louisiana Cultural Vistas.* Barbara Melendez, news coordinator at the University of South Florida, read a draft of the article, providing important critical feedback to produce a reader-friendly manuscript. I am grateful to David Johnson for accepting that piece for publication in *LCV.*

In August 2010, Millisia and I approached the historians at the Louisiana State Museum's Presbytere to discuss the possibility of an exhibition to commemorate the centennial of the tradition, which purportedly began around 1912. We met with Charles Chamberlain and Karen Leathem. They were receptive, citing the compatibility of the exhibition theme with the mission of the museum. Both have expressed and demonstrated their enthusiasm for the exhibition throughout the planning stages. Millisia and I have continued to work on gathering the objects for display, building support in the community for the exhibition, and conducting background research. The exhibition is scheduled to open in early 2013. I would like to thank the Presbytere staff, who are working to make the exhibition a reality: Dawn Deano Hammatt, director of curatorial services; K. Whitney Babineaux, interpretive services director; Karen Trahan Leathem, Louisiana State Museum historian; Katie Harrison, museum special projects coordinator; Jennae Biddiscombe, who coordinates all exhibition-related artifacts for exhibits; Gaynell Brady, K-12 program consultant, who creates and implements gallery-based programs for school audiences; Beth Sherwood, who handles all rights and reproductions; Turry M. Flucker, former community program manager and LSM project director, Louisiana Civil Rights Museum; Patrick Burns, director of exhibits; Greg Lambousy, director of collections; Aimee St. Amant, who coordinates exhibition organization and artifact installation; and Wayne Phillips, curator of costumes and textiles and curator of carnival collections. Christina Barrios developed the exhibition website, which was made possible by a Community Partnership Grant from the New Orleans Jazz and Heritage Festival Foundation.

Millisia and I developed a jazz dance curriculum that we call "Creative Movement from 'Jass' to 'Bounce.'" This curriculum presents a historical overview of the music and dance that enslaved Africans and free people of color developed into the current art form that has become synonymous with New Orleans's culture. The Baby Doll tradition is included as this practice incorporated New Orleans music and dance from its very beginning. We were honored to first share the curriculum with McDonogh 42 Elementary Charter School. I offer thanks to their former staff: Roslyn Smith, president, Tremé Charter School Board of Directors; Cynthia Williams, chief executive officer; Gail Lazard, principal; Carla Lewis, assistant principal; and Donna Stuart, guidance counselor. The art teacher, Aleta Richards, took on the responsibility of reinforcing the lesson and helped the students produce beautiful masks as a culminating activity.

In the summer of 2010 I worked with two University of South Florida undergraduate research assistants, Krysta Ledford and Zachary Cardwell. Zachary was matched with me by Dr. Linda Lucas, director of the National Scholarship Office at the University of South Florida. Krysta began working with me by way of a course she took with me, History of Feminism in the United States, and through the Office of Undergraduate Research. Krysta researched the biographies of photographers past and current who took pictures of the Baby Dolls. Zachary researched obituary and census information for Golden Slipper Social and Pleasure Club members, especially Louis Reimonenq. While I was at the University of South Florida, this work was supported, in part, by the University of South Florida System, Internal Awards Program, Established Researcher Grant, under Grant No. 0020650.

Several reference librarians assisted me in determining whether there were any existing drawings of the Baby Dolls done by Caroline Durieux, artist and director of the Louisiana Federal Arts Project of the Works Progress Administration. I was looking for this source as cited by Jerry Brock in his article on time he spent with the Tremé neighborhood's Happy House Social and Pleasure Club. It turned out that the drawing was done by John McCrady and published in a book co-authored by Durieux. The librarians are Natalie A. Mault, assistant curator, Louisiana State University Museum of Art, Shaw Center for the Arts; Bruce Raeburn, curator of the Hogan Jazz Archives and assistant dean of libraries for special collections, Tulane; Mary Linn Wernet, university archivist and records officer, Cammie G. Henry Research Center Watson Library, Northwestern State University of Louisiana; and Charlene Bonnette, head librarian for Louisiana Collection Preservation, Louisiana Collection, State Library of Louisiana. Charlene also helped with reproduction permissions for photographs of the 1942 Baby Doll celebration.

Matthew Martinez was instrumental in introducing me to Blake Woods, who oversees the John McCrady estate. Both Matthew and Blake were immediately supportive of this project. Blake gave me permission to reproduce the McCrady drawings. I thank Debra Mouton for asking her relatives to verify information regarding her mother, Neliska "Baby" Briscoe, and for sharing additional information from an interview/performance of her mother. As I searched for sources about Arnold Louis Reimonenq, family members Alden Reimonenq and Mark Reimonenq responded to my questions. Mark put me in touch with his aunt Elaine Gutierrez, who has conducted research on the Reimonenq family's genealogy. She offered first-hand memories of her uncle. Ronnie Cressy Rephan, Rudolph Cressy's daughter, provided a rich description of her father and her own memories of her rich relationship with Louis and Fannie Reimonenq. My efforts to discover who held the copyright for Bradley Smith's iconic photos of the Baby Dolls taken on Mardi Gras day around 1938 brought me into contact with numerous people: Daniel Hammer, head of Reader Services, The Historic New Orleans Collection, Williams Research Center; Robert C. Ray, head of Special Collections and University Archives, Library and Information Access, San Diego State University; Wendy S. Israel, manager of editorial operations, Hearst Magazines; and Victor S. Perlman, general counsel and managing director, American Society of Media Photographers. Mara Vivat, who oversees Bradley Smith Productions, was able to provide copyright permission and to give additional information about how Smith interpreted the photographs. I was also assisted by Sharon Smith, Bradley Smith's daughter; and Hannah Flom, Smith's niece. Millisia and I interviewed Joycelyn Green Askew, a descendant of Olivia Green, who was a Baby Doll during the Jazz Age. It is through Joycelyn that we have one of the earliest representations of the costumes of the Baby Dolls. Joycelyn's memories of Olivia helped to give us a picture of the women who were part of this tradition.

The most herculean while gratifying task of all was the effort to identify Robert J. McKinney. I began by contacting the African American *Chicago Defender* and *Louisiana Weekly* newspapers. Identification was muddy and murky until Lester Sullivan, Xavier University of Louisiana archivist, suggested consulting the alumni annals and discovered that McKinney was a 1933 graduate. Lester also knew that 1933 was one of the few years with a yearbook, given that this was during the Depression. Keith Weldon Medley remembered seeing McKinney's name in the course of his research on Ernest Wright, also a 1933 Xavier graduate. But Keith also recalled that his mother spoke of McKinney. Ever the historian, Keith consulted his mother's copy of her McDonogh No. 35 Public High School 1928 and 1929 yearbooks and found more references to McKinney. Soon a picture emerged of this heretofore elusive journalist and ethnographer. I consulted with Beverly Cook, archivist, Chicago Public Library, who located a number of sources that mention McKinney. Other librarians who searched their sources were Alaina W. Hébert, associate curator, Hogan Jazz Archive, Tulane University, and Sean Benjamin, public services librarian, Louisiana Research Collection, Howard-Tilton Memorial Library, Tulane. Mary Linn Wernet, university archivist and records officer, Cammie G. Henry Research Center, Watson Library, Northwestern State University of Louisiana, was instrumental in connecting me with the numerous transcripts Robert McKinney produced. She also located Lyle Saxon's letter to John Davis indicating McKinney's starting date with the Louisiana Writers' Project. In her office, Shelia Thompson willingly culled Robert Tallant's file collections to locate McKinney's work, copied them, and helped with processing.

Others acted as light posts along the way. Irene Wainwright, archivist, Louisiana Division–City Archives, New Orleans Public Library, helped me understand the "Hidden from History: Unknown New Orleanians" exhibition and processed the permissions for use of photographs from that display. Christopher Harter, director of library and reference services, Amistad Research Center at Tulane University, was helpful in reproducing the photograph from the *Louisiana Weekly* and giving a probable identification of the photographer. Sandra Law at the University of South Florida processed numerous interlibrary loan requests. I was happy to meet Girard Mouton III and learn of his enthusiasm for the history of the Baby Doll tradition. Girard had notes on Marcus Christian's reference to the Baby Dolls in his classic poem, "I Am New Orleans." Girard also alerted me to Victor Huber's *Mardi Gras: A Pictorial History of Carnival in New Orleans,* which documents a chant that Baby Dolls sang in Creole patois.

I would also like to acknowledge Dwight Harris, who introduced me to Andrew Justin, Chief of Wild Tremé Mardi Gras Indians, whose mother and other female relatives masked as Baby Dolls during the height of the practice. Andrew introduced me to Denise Trepagnier, who masked with the Ernie K-Doe Baby Dolls, and I thank her for agreeing to be interviewed for this book. I thank Cherice Harrison-Nelson, who initiated an important project documenting women's participation in the Mardi Gras Indian tradition which culminated in the annual Queen's Rule panel, awards, and recognition celebration. I thereby learned about Mercedes Stevenson, Big Queen of Wild Tchoupitoulas, who masked for a time as a Baby Doll and had important eyewitness accounts from uptown New Orleans. I thank her daughter, Mary Kim Stevenson, for assisting with setting up the interview. I had long been intellectually enriched by Maurice Martinez's perspective on the role of culture in bringing a respite from the suffering imposed under segregation, and on how cultural practices can serve as a method of protest when legal remedies failed. I was buoyed by his idea that Black masking practices offer a unique expression of the inner spirit that won't be broken. This work is better because he gave of his time for a long interview.

As though they were calling me home in the midst of writing this book, I honor our foremothers and forefathers for their voices that still echo today through this project. I was privileged to become the associate dean of the College of Arts and Sciences at Xavier University of Louisiana in the summer of 2011. The entire Xavier family has been very supportive. I thank President Norman Francis, who immediately understood the nature of the project in terms of uncovering unhidden history and the significance of preserving this heritage of our city. I thank Anil Kukreja, dean of the College of Arts and Sciences, and Dr. Loren Blanchard, senior vice-president of academic affairs, for supporting this research. Michelle Balan, Dean's Office executive assistant, and Gerald Villavaso, assistant dean, have guided visitors to meetings in our office, processed requests, and been enthusiastic about bringing the book and exhibition into fruition. I am grateful to Professor Ron Bechet for introducing me to the Seventh Ward initiative, The Porch, and sharing photographs of a group of young ladies who masked one year as Baby Dolls, creating a stunning and colorful scene while introducing this tradition to their generation.

Friend and colleague Gary Lemons was with me in the early conceptualization of my scholarly book project on "Sites of Alterity, Pedagogy in Public Places." I found my way to the Baby Doll masking tradition as part of a larger question about where noninstitutionalized knowledge by marginalized people gets created, sustained, enacted, and transformed. Having been raised in New Orleans, I knew well that multiple sites of alternative knowledge production existed. My research on the Baby Dolls was to be a section in a chapter on women and non-heteronormative spaces in New Orleans. Once I met Millisia, my understanding, awe, and respect for this tradition grew. Another friend, Lycia Alexander-Guerra, provided constant support for my work. I thank her for her frequent check-ins, even calling me on Mardi Gras to make sure all was well. Michelle Mitcham made her home and hospitality available as I was pressed to complete the manuscript in the midst of my relocation preparations. I am grateful for her cheerful, insightful, and supportive friendship.

As this research required frequent trips to New Orleans, my dear cousin Sheila Vaz Gaskins and Kenneth Leslie generously made their home available. They checked on me often in evening outings to make sure I was safe. Each drove me around to appointments and accompanied me to many cultural events. Sheila made sure I always had breakfast, dinner, and snacks to take with me while I was on the go. Two other friends, angels really, Yolande Bradley and Cheryl Dejoie-LaCabe, have my eternal gratitude. Yolande opened her home during my many research trips and listened to my formative ideas. Cheryl's generosity and lifelong friendship made this work exciting—not to mention her work on the graphic design for the exhibition brochure. Cheryl can make a stunning second-line umbrella.

Men play unique roles in the masking tradition. While men no longer mask as Baby Dolls (though they are in no way prevented), there are auxiliary roles that continue: serving as musician, masking as a "Skeleton," providing logistics and security, and as oral historians. Calvin "DJ Hektik"

Dyer, Eddie "Duke" Edwards, Cyril Duplesis, and Bruce "Sunpie" Barnes are central to Black masking traditions in New Orleans. A big thank you goes to Desiree Edwards for her hospitality in Edgard, Louisiana, when I interviewed her father. Royce Osborn has shared many resources, ideas, and connections, proving that he is a true colleague.

I thank Margaret Lovecraft, acquisitions editor at Louisiana State University Press, for making the publication process smooth. I am also grateful to Stan Ivester for his editorial efforts, which yielded a better manuscript.

The Baby Dolls themselves have contributed much to this research, making this practice come alive for me and for the readers of this book. They are Miriam Batiste Reed, Mercedes Stevenson, Geannie Thomas, Tee-Eva Perry, Denise Trepagnier, Karen Harris, Lois Nelson, Merline Kimble, Patricia McDonald, Tammy Montana, and Resa "Cinnamon Black" Wilson-Bazile. A special thank you is extended to Miriam Reed, whose deep involvement and knowledge about the practice allowed its hidden and easily overlooked elements to become visible.

The following 2010 New Orleans Society of Dance members graciously participated in a group interview for the *Louisiana Cultural Vistas* article: Diana "Lady MamaCita" Calix-Harvard, Kenethia "Lady N.O. Cutie" Morgan, Toya "504's Finest" Payne-Smith, and Akella "Baby Doll Lady 9thWD Shortie" Norton. I learned from the 2012 company members as I was a participant-observer to their performance in the Zulu Social and Pleasure Club annual parade: Sara Green, Diamond Lawrence, Kashonna Conner, Juliana Wagner, Moriah Dyer, Whitney Dickerson, Ayanna Barham, Diana Calix-Harvard, Keah Moffett, Shekevia Bickham, Rennekia Goffney, and Kenethia Morgan. Finally, I would also like to thank the 2012 New Orleans Society of Dance's Honorary Baby Doll Ladies for helping me to experience the pleasure of sisterhood through pageantry: Mia Gonzales, Joycelyn Green Askew, Charmagne Andrews, Marietta Robertson, Luliana "Lana" Mars, Linda Morgan, Heidi Thomas, Fabieyoun Walker, Yolanda Wilson, Rita Amedee, Kashonna Conner, Dolly Eaglin, Sherri Clark, Shenae Clark, Omika Williams, Michelle Briscoe-Long, Karla Ray, Janna Zinzi, Chicava H. Child, and Alana Harris.

APPENDIX A

A History of Baby Doll Masking in the Baby Dolls' Own Words

ORIGINS OF THE TRADITION

The following quotations reveal the origins of the Baby Doll tradition. While popular sources have told the first half of the story, about a group of uptown women organizing for a singular event, full quotations from the women themselves reveal how these women who were familiar with organizing drew on their strengths and disciplined themselves into a group that followed the regular norms of social and pleasure clubs.

Sure they all call me Baby Doll, that's my name. They have been calling me Baby Doll for a long time. I guess eighteen years. How I come to get that name? Well, I'll tell you.

I don't know if I can take credit for organizing the Baby Dolls you asked me about, but I know I have always been a Baby Doll. I'm a Baby Doll today and every day a Baby Doll. A bunch of us got together way back eighteen years ago, I was just twenty years old. Since I was always dressed as a Baby Doll the other girls said they would dress like me. They would wear tight skirts with bloomers and a rimmed hat.

We use to meet in a room and dress at the same time. Sometimes we would lug our clothes to the house where we met the night before. This was done because a lot of our husbands and old men didn't want us to be Baby Dolls because they knew a lot of men would follow us on the street and try to make mashes on [have sex with] us. We didn't tell them how we were going to mask but just came out as a Baby Doll. And boy was we tight!?

We use to sing, clap our hands, and you know what people call raddy? Well, that's the way we use to walk down the street.
—*Clara Belle Moore, as told to Robert McKinney, February 9, 1940*

Here is what happened in 1912. Ida Jackson, Millie Barnes, and Sallie Gail and a few other gals downtown was making up to mask on Mardi Gras day. I don't know how they were going to mask, but they were going to mask. Well, I wasn't good at forming a club so I told Leola Tate. . . . Old Lizzie and Leola got all the gals together. . . . We wouldn't drink because we wanted to talk and get something done.

Leola and all of us were sitting around. The room was packed. Leola who use to belong to the church and one of the helping hands associations and who use to go to all those meetings, said, "Come to order." And we came to order. She said "What is your pleasure?" We didn't have one but we had a motion and an object. I raised that by saying we wanted to mask up in an association for Mardi Gras to outdo all [Black women] maskers. Somebody says that is fine and what are we going to call ourselves. A gal named Althea Brown said let's be ourselves, let's be Baby Dolls, that's what the pimps call us. That suited everybody and then we went into motion. This was in 1912, the year the Baby Dolls started. We started coming up with money. Leola said, hold your horses. Let every tub stand on its own bottom. That suited everybody and the tubs stood.

Everybody agreed to have fifty dollars in her stocking and that we would see who could have the most money, that was fine. Somebody says what is the name of our association, and we said let's call it the Million Dollar Baby Dolls and be red hot. Yes, indeed, we went out and got us some rainbow colors, panel backs and panel fronts made out of gold lace. Leola Tate was our head leader. No we ain't had nothing to do with the Zulus. Old Johnny Metoyer wanted us to come along with them but we wouldn't do it. We told Johnny we were out to do up some fun in our own way and we were not stopping at nothing, no indeed. Yes sir, the Zulus had their gang and we had ours.

Some of us made our dresses and some of us had them made. We were all looking sharp. There were thirty of us. . . . We were all good looking and had our stuff with us. Man, I'm telling you we had money all over us, even in our bloomers, and they didn't have any zips.

And Mardi Gras day came and we hit the streets. I'm telling you we hit the streets looking forty and fine and mellow. We got out about 10:15. We had stacks of dollars in our stockings and in our hand. We went to Sam Bonart playground on Rampart and Poydras and bucked up against each other to see who had the most money. Leola had the most money; she had $102. I had $96 and I was second, but I had more money at home in case I ran out. There wasn't a woman in the bunch who had less than $50. No, I don't guess we had a million dollars but we had a hell of a lot of money.

. . . We went on downtown and talking about putting on the ritz. . . . We were smoking cigars and flinging ten and twenty dollar bills through the air. Sure, we use to sing, and boy did we shake on down. What we sang? We sang "When the Sun goes down" and "When the saints come marching through I want to be in that number."

. . . When we hit downtown all the girls couldn't do anything but look at us. They had to admit that we were stuff. . . . And there you have the starting of the Baby Dolls. Yeah, peace was made. All of the girls got together.

Leola went out and got a band. We had to pay two-fifty apiece for that. She got sign carriers. We had to pay a half-dollar apiece for that. That's all the public expense I think we had, because there must have been more but Leola took care of that. We gave her money.

. . . Our band was made up of a cornet player, a flute player, drummer, and banjo player. The men made good music. Man, we wore those wide hats, and they were seldom worn because we got hot and pulled them off. I'm telling you that when the Million Dollar Baby Dolls strutted, they strutted, I'm telling you.

We on down the years never did ask help from anybody. In 1914 I. W. Harper Whiskey took some of our expense because we advertised their whiskey. We met every Sunday, we had a social club and paid dues, ten cents a week. We took care of our expense on Mardi Gras by taxing our members two and a half a head. Man and we never failed to have our green money with us or do our shaking on the street.

Of course we couldn't keep our association. Some of got sick, some of them dropped out, but the Million Dollar Baby Dolls went on.

—*Beatrice Hill, as told to Robert McKinney, March 11, 12, 14, 1940*

THREAT TO THE TRADITION

Along with the Mardi Gras Indians, Baby Dolls turned out on St. Joseph's feast night in full masked attire. No one knows exactly how the masking began, but by 1940 it was clearly a long-established and well-anticipated event. The moral authority of the Catholic Church had gotten fed up with the seeming desecration of the saint's day and proposed that the maskers use some secular day to have their fun.

Captain Jackson Keeps the Baby Dolls from Strutting Their Stuff

St. Joseph night was clear, slightly chilly, but perfectly swell for mirth, especially Baby Doll fun. This is the night that is usually a second Mardi Gras for a lot of people, i.e., Baby Dolls and their ilk. They mask and wave their hips, sing low down blues songs to the accompaniment of loud cornets, banjos, drums and other instruments. They frolic on the streets much in the same manner as they do on Fat Tuesday; their shimmies are strictly solid and always attract large crowds.

In their minds, they had built up St. Joseph night as "the biggest night we ever had"; they had re-pressed their long-waisted, pleated skirts of bright colors and had turned enough tricks to have green backs in their stockings. Nothing was going to stop the baby Dolls, not even a storm. "There is always an inside."

Well, there was no storm, but something happened that was much worse, its effects are still being felt and promulgated. The Archbishop stepped into the picture and said there should not be any masking because it fell in the Lenten Season. He suggested April 2 instead. Like Jennie Watts said, "Who is the Archbishop? He ain't none of our pappy," and she is a Baby Doll whose attitudes about most things is definitely indifferent. Because the Archbishop made himself clear in the matter, Captain Jackson of the First Precinct sent out a word that there must be no masking, only a few Baby Dolls accepted his message; they promised to mask and were going to do so. They were so persistent the usually calm police captain became irate and contacted them himself. Baby Irene, some kind of dictator in Baby Doll affairs, stated, "The Captain says, 'I don't want no masking, and if any of you do, so I'm going put your black asses in jail.' Cause, I personally wouldn't give a fuck, but I don't feel like going back to jail. I just got out."

A large crowd was on hand, around Poydras and Saratoga streets, the cradle of dope, to watch the Baby Dolls do their stuff amid a "glory" that is somewhat shameful to an aristocratic eye but is good entertainment. Fancy-colored music boxes were playing while women and men danced gleefully. . . .

. . . Baby Irene merely said, "Lord today! Here is the man who is going to make our picture. I'd be sailing if it don't be for Captain Jackson. What he's got to do with it? The captain says if we come out masking he's going put our black asses in the hoose. Lord today. Ain't this something?" Another Baby Doll rushed from the corner to say, "Our fun is all fucked up."

There were only three masked Baby Dolls present: their rusty legs peeped from under short, satin skirts which were tight around their posteriors. Masking was very light among some of the Baby Dolls for the first time in twenty years. One of the more peppery Baby Dolls said she didn't give a damn what the Archbishop said she was going to mask, and she did so. This dishpan-faced Baby Doll must have been charged with a "weed" cigarette (she was certainly "togged" down in a short red skirt with a cowboy-like hat) because she left the scene literally walking on air, stating, "I'm going to the Tick Tock and I'm high as a kite." Somebody chided, "You ain't never get in no Tick Tock, that's high class nigger winch." The "chick" laughed, but changed her mind about going to the Tick Tock.

—*Robert McKinney, March 19, 1940*

THE MANY FACES OF THE BABY DOLLS

New Orleans author Harnett Kane captured one group of Baby Dolls that followed the District's script. The other quotes that follow from Mercedes Stevenson, Allison Montana, and Miriam Batiste Reed reveal aspects of the masking tradition that have been overlooked and ignored. These non–District-related maskers recalled their neighbors having fun with the Baby Doll tradition and how it surfaced in mainstream Black communities as a way to make a statement about the importance of having fun and showing oneself off in a world that would otherwise belittle them.

How to enjoy it [Mardi Gras] best? Most New Orleanians would suggest that you be up early, about eight or so to see Zulu at the New Basin Canal and follow him for a time. . . . For early afternoon masking, the Orleanian will recommend the Canal Street business section. . . . You might try North Claiborne Ave. for the remarkable "Indians"—Negros in ornate and lavish disguise; or the "Baby Dolls"—dark girls of more than good will.

—*Harnett Kane,* Queen New Orleans: City by the River (*New York: William T. Morrow & Co., 1949*)

When I was coming up, there were three ladies in our neighborhood who were best friends: Geneva Tapps, Martha Tapps, and Mozella masked as Baby Dolls. I use to watch them. They would be so much fun. They would be in those short dresses. They had bloomers underneath and they would pull their dresses up. We would follow them to the white bar room. The owner would open up the doors to them because it was Carnival. They would dance on the counter.

—*Mercedes Stevenson, March 26, 2011, referring to late 1930s and early 1940s Twelfth Ward, uptown*

The first year we dressed my friends Caroline, Eloise, and I dressed in pants I sewed. Caroline's color was pink, Eloise's color was green, and mine was gold. We decided we weren't going to do this next year. We decided to dress as Baby Dolls. Carol said "what are we going to do with our shoes?" We got a clear [material like a table cloth] and fixed them up. We made the bonnets from like a long time ago. We wore short dresses with a pinafore that had a bow in the back. We wore socks like the babies. Everybody would say, "Oh here come the baby dolls."

—*Mercedes Stevenson, March 26, 2011, referring to early 1970s*

I've been making masks for more than forty years. I know how to make all the outfits. I can make the skeleton outfit, the baby doll outfit (with black shirts, pink blouses with puffed sleeves, black mask, a black whip, black boots). The men with the Baby Dolls would take two pairs of shoes and make one out of them so they'd be twice as long. I masked with the Baby Dolls about twice, and then I masked with the skeleton about three times before I masked Indians.

During my early years they had the Rosebud Social and Pleasure Club—women who use to mask. Even all the gay people use to mask. They dressed in women's clothes, expensive lace and stockings. Men use to mask as women, and there were even women who would mask as men. The masks were made out of screen wire. The Million Dollar Babies were women who had money, ten, twenty, and fifty dollar bills in their stockings.

—*Allison "Tootie" Montana, quoted in Michael Proctor Smith,*
A Joyful Noise: A Celebration of New Orleans Music
(Dallas: Taylor Publications, 1990)

The Baby Dolls were started by the Batiste family. We were on the 1300th block of St. Phillip Street. Our house was called the big house. My mother, Alma Batiste, had her club named the Golden Slipper. I remember them masking as Baby Dolls. They would go to each other's houses to make their costumes.

The Baby Doll costumes were made of satin, green red blue, pink, and white. I can recall a lot of the women masked as Baby Dolls with my mother's club Golden Slipper; I can only give you nicknames because I was small. The Batiste family from St. Phillip, my mother and them, they were out there masking the Baby Dolls, the Skeletons, the Indians, and the Dirty Dozen were organized from the Batiste family.

My mother and them would come out early as the Dirty Dozen as early in the morning as 4:30–5:00 AM. The Dirty Dozen was nicknaming how the older people would come out. The men mostly liked to dress in women's clothes. They would put a pillow in the front and a pillow in the back. They had on bonnets.

Later in the day, they would mask as Baby Dolls and go to different houses to stop and have a little recess. They paraded around St. Bernard, Claiborne, Orleans and St. Claude, St. Phillip St. and Dumaine.

—*Miriam Batiste Reed, April 22, 2010, referring to*
the late 1930s to early 1940s

If you wanted to be a Baby Doll with the original Baby Dolls, you have to dress like the Baby Dolls, in the years that I had it, you know. We would parade in the street and stop at different houses. And everybody would be out there: "Oh, the Baby Dolls is coming, the Baby Dolls is coming."

Well, I love to sing, too. And I'm an old Creole, OK, so when we sing what we don't know the words to something, we go "La la la la la la." So the house that we would stop by, they would have cold drinks for you, and red beans and rice, you know. And you could have something to eat, and then we'd just go along, you know.

—*Interview with Miriam Batiste Reed, by Noah Bonaparte Pais,*
Gambit: Blog of New Orleans, *2009*

REVIVING THEIR PARENTS' TRADITIONS

The masking traditions of bygone days were so important to later generations that they began to revive the revelry making of their ancestors. Families like the Batistes and the Phillipses were well known for creating fun and merriment for themselves, their neighbors, and their community. To honor their ancestors and to celebrate in classic style, many descendants picked up the family customs after they had been dormant for some time.

We met at 7 AM at Felicia Shezbie's house on Orleans Avenue. A huge breakfast with eggs, pork chops, gumbo, biscuits, gravy, greens, rice and desserts was the morning meal.

Following breakfast Precisely Batiste led a prayer for our safety and to have a beautiful day. Then we hit the streets.

We paraded from 8 AM Fat Tuesday until 2 AM the following morning. There was a loosely organized route with rest periods. We strutted through huge crowds on Claiborne with ease and grace. They played old ribald songs, jazz tunes, and Creole songs. Everyone loved the Baby Dolls, and thousands of revelers cleared a path for the Baby Dolls and the Dirty Dozen.

In the middle of a gigantic crowd, a space would magically open and there would be a three-legged card table barely standing with a fifth of Jack Daniels for the Baby Dolls and Dozen. It was more surreal than a Fellini film. The next stop might be gumbo and sandwiches.

A lesser-known but striking group of Baby Dolls from further downtown were known as Satan (spelled Satin) and Sinners. Film footage shows Satan with his red union drawers and with white cotton boxers worn outside. Along with his long red tail and his red horns he carried a decorated umbrella. A man carried a sign saying "Satin and Sinners," and the Baby Dolls followed three abreast strutting in red satin baby doll outfits.

Others have claimed that the Baby Dolls were just prostitutes who masked on Mardi Gras. But that seriously oversimplifies it. They were hard working people caught up in the life they were dealt but made the most of. They stuck together and created an ironic twist unlike any other.

These people, born into a repressed condition, turned it around and made a brilliant creation of live art. The joy they spread changed the path of culture worldwide. The Baby Dolls were a welcome and unique part of an African-American renaissance centered in New Orleans.

—*Jerry Brock, "The Million Dollar Baby Dolls,"*
New Orleans Beat Street *2, no. 2*

When my sister Felicia died, I had someone to get a mannequin. I dressed that mannequin in a Baby Doll dress and bonnet and socks. My sister was laid out at Charbonnet's funeral home and that mannequin was standing at the head of her casket. They had jazz funerals for my sisters as well as my brothers.

—*Interview with Miriam Batiste Reed, April 22, 2010*

Merline Kimble has been an active member of the Gold Diggers since 1985. The original Gold Diggers' Baby Dolls have a history that dates back to the 1900s, she says, adding that her grandmother Louise Recasner Phillips was an original member of the Gold Diggers' Baby Dolls.

According to stories passed down to Kimble, the Gold Diggers would come out as early as two in the morning, and hundreds of people would be waiting outside her grandmother's house on Dumaine Street. On Mardi Gras day the Gold Diggers Baby Dolls can still be found on Dumaine Street, in the heart of the Tremé.

"Being a Baby Doll gives you the opportunity to do all the crazy things that you would not normally do," Kimble says. "I am a very conservative lady, but when you put the baby doll costume on you become another person. People scream 'baby doll, baby doll, baby doll' and all sorts of things happen. It is a lot of fun."

—*Theresa Crushshon, "Oh Baby: New Orleans Baby Doll Tradition*
Thrives," New Orleans Tribune, *2010*

ERNIE K-DOE BABY DOLLS: ON BECOMING A NEW ORLEANS ICON

Newcomers to New Orleans begin their understanding of the Baby Dolls with Antoinette K-Doe's push to revive the tradition. Steeped in the culture of entertainment via the neighborhood lounge, Antoinette catapulted herself to fame, as had the original Baby Dolls, through the use of bravado, making a scene, and stealing the show. Not content to be known as the wife of Ernie K-Doe, Antoinette was determined to make a name for herself. The death of her husband, a well-known local rhythm-and-blues singer, left her bereft and with a club to promote without the legendary figure at her side. In honoring his memory, she looked for ways to continue having his name and the name of their lounge in the public eye. The Baby Dolls served that need and, because of it, the Baby Doll masking tradition enjoyed a resurgence.

Antoinette noticed that Allison "Tootie" Montana's portrait was not painted on the pilings under the Claiborne Avenue bridge like the other Mardi Gras Indians. Ernie K-Doe's portrait was under the bridge. She said Ernie should not have been under the bridge because he was a rhythm-and-blues singer and not a Mardi Gras Indian. She got permission from Tootie's wife to paint his image on the outside of the Mother-in-Law Lounge, which she owned. Antoinette remembered that the Baby Dolls marched with the Indians and wanted to be part of that tradition. We said that we were going to be the Ernie K-Doe Baby Dolls, Antoinette, Tee-Eva, and me. We didn't know what to do so we called Ms. Miriam Batiste Reed.

—*Interview with Geannie Thomas, an Ernie K-Doe*
Baby Doll, April 25, 2010

[Miriam Batiste Reed] brought all her dresses, her bonnets. She remembered how to cut out a newspaper pattern for the bonnets. She taught us how to do the dresses. I caught on real quickly because I'm a seamstress. When that year was over, she showed me how to make the Baby Doll dresses out of crepe paper. I keep saying I'm going to do one out of crepe paper and put it in a glass cabinet and put in somewhere in here. Don't ask me where.

The walk, the dance—it's more like a strut. Miss Miriam grew up in a musical family, the Batistes. She said when the Baby Dolls would go out they would make their little tambourines. She gave me the pattern, and I had some guys make some tambourines. So we all had our little tambourines. When we get out there, wherever Northside Skull and Bones Gang Chief Bruce "Sunpie" Barnes takes us is where that old music happens for the Baby Dolls. And we all be together having fun. When Zulu gets on this end, we get with Zulu, we just get out there. Just have fun.

—Antoinette K-Doe, quoted by Noah Bonaparte Pais, "R.I.P. Antoinette K-Doe," Gambit: Blog of New Orleans, *2009*

The Baby Dolls had disappeared, and I brought the Baby Dolls back. I named them the Ernie K-Doe Baby Dolls. The reason I did that was to show the new Baby Dolls are career ladies. We all working ladies. The history of Baby Dolls, from years ago when I was a little girl, I thought they were baby dolls that I could play with. My grandmother told me, "No, it's ladies." It developed into getting history on the Baby Dolls, because I was always fascinated by our culture. And I understood that the Baby Dolls was whores. I knew they had the Red Light District, the Baby Dolls here. So when I brought the Baby Dolls back, I didn't want them to have the reputation they had before. I said, "You know what? Let's clean up the act." So we made it career ladies.

The next year, they had some Baby Dolls wanted to join us, 2005. I told them, "Listen. Y'all can join us, it's fine. But there will not be a disgrace on these Baby Dolls." Because we grandmothers, we parents, whatever. We have our life to live after Mardi Gras. So they didn't like the rules that I had fixed for my Baby Dolls: to wear clothes but wear them decent, not with everything showing. Ms. Miriam Batiste told me, "Antoinette, they had another set of Baby Dolls, over here in the black Mardi Gras area, called the Gold Diggers."

—Antoinette K-Doe, quoted by Pais, "R.I.P. Antoinette K-Doe"

We have to set ourselves apart from those other Baby Dolls. The Ernie K-Doe Baby Dolls were the last big group. There were thirty-five to forty of us that marched with Tootie that Mardi Gras. Not long after that, he dropped dead fighting for the Indians gathering under the bridge.

—Interview with Geannie Thomas, April 25, 2010

The Ernie K-Doe Baby Dolls were pallbearers for the funeral of Lloyd Washington. He was one of the last living members of the Ink Spots vocal group. His wife, Hazel, had no way to bury him or no money for a hearse. We used my red Dodge Dakota truck and decorated it with greenery. Antoinette had kept his ashes in her lounge, the Mother-in-Law, for months until a burial place could be found for him. We had a casket we used as a stage prop in theatrical performances we did. So Miriam Batiste Reed, Tee-Eva, Antoinette, and Lollipop and I marched all the way to the cemetery. We marched from St. Augustine Catholic Church to St. Louis Cemetery Number One on Basin Street. I carried Hazel in my truck. People said they had not seen women pallbearers, especially for such a legend as Lloyd Washington. We wore black dresses with white birds on our shoulders.

—*Interview with Geannie Thomas, April 25, 2010*

It is an honor to be a Baby Doll. When I was coming up, I always loved dolls but we were very poor. My mother had three girls. At Christmas we got candy, but never a doll. I was ten years old when my grandfather must have helped my mother buy a doll for me. I will never forget the velvet skirt. I loved that doll. And now to be able to be a Baby Doll and for other people to look and say, "Wow you look good, you are a Baby Doll," is a thrill. When we marched the first year, people said, "The Baby Dolls! We remember." So many people said they remembered. When we came down Canal Street the crowd was so happy to see the Baby Dolls were back. They said they remembered their grandparents being Baby Dolls. Little kids would say, "Oh momma that is a BD." "Mama, who is that Baby Doll?" Any time I put the dress on I am as excited as the first day. I am still happy to be a Baby Doll. It represents the doll I was never able to have, and it represents being with Antoinette and things she got me into.

—*Interview with Geannie Thomas, April 25, 2010*

The frilly clothes, bows, the baby doll shoes the Baby Dolls wear are like being a little lady. It is real cute and it takes you back. When I was a little girl in Hansville in St. Charles Parish, the adults use to dress us up in fancy and frilly dresses to go to church. I was always dressed liked a doll. Our church had an association that organized a band and a parade. I loved the band. If I heard something beat, I would go. I was always a leader and would hold the banner for the name of the church. I was always in the front of the parade. I am still the leader of the pack.

—*Interview with Eva Perry, an Ernie K-Doe Baby Doll, April 25, 2010*

One hundred years ago, when it would be Mardi Gras time, the women in New Orleans they would get dressed and go out early in the morning. The skull heads would come out, the Indians would come next, and then the Baby Dolls. The Baby Dolls would have flouncy clothes. Very short skirts, bloomers, lace stocking and garters on their legs. Back then they were hustlers; that's what the Baby Dolls were. They went out to make money on a Mardi Gras Day. That's why they went out early because they knew people were coming out to see the Indians. Men would put money in their garter and they made sure that dress was short enough for the men to see the garter and the men knew what they meant having that fancy garter on their leg. When we originated having the Baby Dolls we changed that thing around. We got all professional ladies and ladies who owned businesses. Antoinette K-Doe wanted to keep Ernie K-Doe's name out there. We became the Ernie K-Doe Baby Dolls. We got with Ms. Batiste and learned the history and made the customs. But we would do it differently by doing the things for charity. We have functions amongst ourselves. We don't raise money, we put money up. It is to keep the Baby Dolls alive, but we changed the actions of the Baby Dolls.

—*Interview with Eva Perry, April 25, 2010*

There's a great story Antoinette K-Doe told me about (Ms.) Lollipop bringing her dress to Houston after Hurricane Katrina. You're evacuating a hurricane, you're lucky to bring your toothbrush, and she brought her Baby Doll outfit with her. Anyway, everybody at the shelter was depressed, so to cheer them up she decided to put on her Baby Doll outfit and second-line in the crowd. And somebody yelled out to her, "Hey lady, put some clothes on!"

—*Robert Florence,* New Orleans Cemeteries: Life in the Cities of the Dead, *quoted in Noah Bonaparte Pais, "Rally of the Dolls," February 16, 2009,* Gambit, *www.bestofneworleans.com/gambit/rally-of-the-*dolls/ Content?oid=1256917

SURVIVING THE STORM: RENEWING SPIRITS
AND CREATING NEW TRADITIONS

The song lyric "We made it through the water, the muddy, muddy water," by the Free Agents Brass Band, is a post-Katrina anthem. Along their parade route, the New Orleans Society of Dance's Baby Doll Ladies perform to this selection. In fact, the events surrounding and following Hurricane Katrina are what propelled Millisia White and her brother DJ Hektik to create the dance company. The New Orleans Society of Dance uses aspects of New Orleans's culture, music, dance, and costuming to inspire and encourage members of the community. Among the first to mask after Katrina were Lois Nelson and Merline Kimble, who reassembled the Gold Diggers. Adapting evening gowns for their masking, they demonstrated the resilience characteristic of the original Baby Dolls: out of nothing, create something.

> After Katrina and we came back home, it was me, Pat, Deja, and Cinnamon. We all participated in the Armstrong parade celebration. We didn't have fabric to make the satin dresses. There was nowhere for us to get anything so we dealt with what we had. Cinnamon had evening dresses. Pat became a grandma baby doll. We took the evening gowns and cut them and made them short. We took the part that we cut off from the evening gown and made the bloomers. We weren't dressed like you see Wanda and Merline dressed, we were dressed more up-to-date. We sprayed our hats. Then we went back to the tradition and come out like we use to come out with the bonnet and the bloomers.
>
> —*Interview with Lois Nelson, Gold Digger Baby Dolls, April 25, 2010*

Going through the experience of Hurricane Katrina taught me to submit to and praise God. The message I got is that we are hopeless, but we still thanked God in the midst of it. Some people can't fathom how to sing and praise him in the midst of Katrina. That is where I pulled all of my cultural understanding and my spiritual together. I came back to New Orleans and that is what inspired the "Resurrection," not just of the Baby Dolls, but my desire to promote New Orleans music, song, and dance in general. It was to be *an example of hope.* This is our testimony. We want people to share their testimony. What do you feel you want to resurrect about New Orleans culture? What is your contribution to the resurrection? We motivate and give people a reason why we should hold on to what makes us different and unique.

I wanted to take my experience to the next level and found a dance company. That is how the New Orleans Society of Dance was formed. It is typical for a dance company to have a face or a theme. We took our theme . . . from practices from "back in the day," which is our birthright. We borrow from the idea and contribute to the idea. Everyone's neighborhood had a group of Baby Dolls. It was womanhood personified. To do the tradition justice we consulted with the elders and, with the blessing of past generations of Baby Dolls, we cultivate it, upgrade it, and bring it to 2012.

—*Interview with Millisia White, founder, New Orleans Society of Dance's Baby Doll Ladies, and "Lady Bee," April 22, 2010*

APPENDIX B
Some Known Million Dollar Baby Doll Participants

Name	Description	Source
Beatrice Hill	Went to Leola Tate to help organize masking association for Black women in the Back o' Town District—"to out do" all of them.	Robert McKinney, March 1940
Ida Jackson Milli Barnes Sallie Gail	Uptown women who served as the impetus in 1912 for the downtown women to mask as Baby Dolls.	Beatrice Hill
Leola Tate	Served as de facto leader and organizer of the Million Dollar Baby Dolls Social and Pleasure Club.	Beatrice Hill
Lizzie Barnes	A well-regarded acquaintance of Beatrice who assisted Leola in arranging the organizing meeting of the Million Dollar Baby Dolls Social and Pleasure Club.	Beatrice Hill
Althea Brown	Suggested the name "Baby Dolls"	Beatrice Hill
Willie Brooks	Grand marshal	Beatrice Hill

APPENDIX C

The Geographical Landscape of the Million Dollar Baby Doll

Place Name	Location	Notes
Sam Bonart	Rampart and Poydras streets	Where the Baby Dolls held their "bucking" contest
Silver Platter	Liberty and Thalia streets	After-hours spot for jazz lovers and musicians after working in dance halls; one of several places (including Elites and Black and Tan) where Baby Dolls would dress up and spend money
Entertainers	Franklin Street near Customhouse (1902–early 1930s); well-known jazz artists played there	A bar where Baby Dolls acted out their rivalries over men, money, and their fashionable clothes
Elite (mid-1920s)	Iberville Street between Rampart and Burgundy	A nightclub
Black Storyville, the vice district established by the same city ordinance that established Storyville	Liberty and Gravier streets, South Rampart Street	A collection of bars, dance halls, cribs, and residences; the designated section for Black sex workers to ply their trade
Geddes & Willis		Baby Dolls used their limousines when they wanted to make a statement about their value and worth in the eyes of female rivals; also known to have waited for the Zulu Social Aid and Pleasure Club to arrive at this "toasting" spot

APPENDIX D
Million Dollar Baby Doll Slang

Term	Meaning
Boiling words	Words intended to provoke a fight.
Bucking contest	Competition with rival groups on Carnival Day to see who had the most money within and between gangs of women.
Joint	A bar.
Kick them up	Refers to an erotic dance move.
Lemon	A method of stealing money from a customer when he was sexually occupied with a sex worker. She was in on the scheme.
Mash	To have sex; "masher" means womanizer.
Mask	To wear a costume on Carnival Day.
Rats	Terms used by downtown women in the District to refer to uptown Black women because they were seen as being involved in and/or addicted to drugs.
Red hot	The new jazz music of the time was considered "hot" and was aimed at stimulating couples' sensual dancing.
Ratty vs. Raddy	"Raddy" means you don't give a damn. "Ratty" means you do "rat things," like getting in trouble, going to of jail.
Walking raddy	Erotic walking.
Shake on down	Refers to a type of sensual athletic dance.

Term	Meaning
Show their linen	To display one's underwear publicly in an effort to titillate a potential customer or show up a rival female competitor.
Show out loud	To wear no underwear.
"Tight," "Put on the ritz," "Looking sharp," and "Looking forty and fine and mellow"	Words and phrases the women used to describe how good they looked and the impact of their masking on female competitors and potential male customers.
Uptown/downtown	Sections of the city divided by Canal Street.

APPENDIX E
Charting the History of Baby Doll Groups

Group Name	Approximate Years of Mardi Gras Masking	Mardi Gras Activity
MILLION DOLLAR BABY DOLLS		
Million Dollar Baby Dolls	ca. 1912–1950s	Paraded together, "walking ratty," "shake dancing," singing traditional Creole songs and blues, turning tricks, drinking, smoking reefer. Started and caused street fights with brick throwing and razor flashing.
BABY DOLL MASKING BY SOCIAL AND PLEASURE CLUBS		
Golden Slipper Baby Dolls	ca. 1930s–1950s	Went from house to house of the members of the club, where they received a little "recess" of food and drink. They paraded with the Dirty Dozen Kazoo Band.

Attire	Social and Pleasure Club	Some Known Active Participants	Source
Short pleated skirts; bloomers with ruffles and bows, waists, or halters; poke bonnets; socks or stockings held up by garters for securing dollar bills; cosmetics (e.g., rouge); wigs of corkscrew curls in various colors such as blonde; costumes in pink or blue. Aim was to look as innocent as possible.	Yes	Althea Brown Beatrice Hill	Robert J. McKinney, "The History of the Baby Dolls"
Women and men in colorful shiny satin short dresses, with bonnets, bloomers, baby doll shoes, accessorized with lollipops and screen masks covering their faces or a satin mask with a piece of cloth covering their mouths.	Yes	Alma T. Batiste Louis Reimonenq Fannie Reimonenq Alma Borden	Miriam Batiste Reed

Group Name	Approximate Years of Mardi Gras Masking	Mardi Gras Activity
Gold Diggers	ca. 1930s–1950s	Paraded in the Tremé, going from bar to bar
Rosebud Social and Pleasure Club	ca. 1930s–1950s	Unknown
Satin Sinners	unknown	

REVIVALS

Group Name	Approximate Years of Mardi Gras Masking	Mardi Gras Activity
Batiste Family Baby Dolls and Dirty Dozen Kazoo Band	1970s–1980	Early morning breakfast, prayer, and then paraded along a loosely organized route in the Sixth Ward with rest periods to eat food residents prepared and left on tables. They played old ribald songs, jazz tunes, and Creole songs.
Mercedes Stevenson and Friends	1970s (three years)	
Gold Digger Baby Dolls	possibly discontinuous years but revived periodically, in recent times for the Satchmo Salute Parade	Parade in the Tremé neighborhood.

Attire	Social and Pleasure Club	Some Known Active Participants	Source
Women wore satin dresses trimmed with fur, cork-screw curls, and carried canes. Men wore top hats and "dress suits" in the same color as the women, and carried canes; some dressed as police officers.	Yes	Louise R. Phillips Octave Phillips	Merline Kimble
"The women dressed up as baby dolls in black tights and pink accessories. The men wore derbies and bow ties."	Yes	Allison Montana	Turner, *Jazz Religion, the Second Line, and Black New Orleans*
Satin dresses; men wore devil costumes.	Yes	Anita Thomas	Sylvester Francis Backstreet Museum, New Orleans
Short satin dress, bloomers, poke bonnet, baby bottles, pacifiers, baby dolls.	Yes (Happy House)	Felicia Batiste Shezbie Miriam Batiste Reed Precisely Batiste	Brock, "Million-Dollar Baby Dolls"
Short satin dresses, bloomers, bonnets and socks.	No	Mercedes Stevenson	Mercedes Stevenson
Costumes vary from "Little Bo-Peep" to traditional satin with bloomers, pacifiers, lollipops, tambourines, umbrellas.	Unknown	Merline Kimble Resa "Cinnamon Black" Wilson-Bazile Wanda Pearson Janice Kimble Tammy Montana Sherrie Roboteaux Lois Nelson Patricia McDonald Deja Andrews	Merline Kimble

Group Name	Approximate Years of Mardi Gras Masking	Mardi Gras Activity
Ernie K-Doe Baby Dolls	2004	Paraded in Tremé, notably on Claiborne Ave.; for first outing, were led by Northside Skull and Bones Gang members. Met up with the Indians and the Zulus before returning to the Mother-in-Law Lounge.
Tremé Million Dollar Baby Dolls	2010–present	Most notably Satchmo Festival every August and at jazz funerals.

RESURRECTING THE TRADITION

Millisia White's Baby Doll Ladies, New Orleans Society of Dance	2005–present	Showcase Creole and contemporary second-line dancing in the Zulu Social Aid and Pleasure Club annual parade.

Attire	Social and Pleasure Club	Some Known Active Participants	Source
Women and men wore short baby doll dresses in pastel colors with bonnets, gloves, bloomers, stockings, and garters.	No	Antoinette K-Doe Geannie Thomas Eva Perry Resa "Cinnamon Black" Wilson-Bazile Karen Harris Prudence Grissom Sally Young Denise Trepagnier	Geannie Thomas Eva Perry
Short sexy attire, stockings, garters, pacifiers, tambourines, umbrellas.		Resa "Cinnamon Black" Wilson-Bazile Margie Perez Bec Hunter Milana Jones Carolina Gallop	
Short sexy attire, in black or white, stockings, garters with play money, decorative face paint, curly wigs, tambourines, umbrellas.	No	Millisia "Lady Bee" White Diana "Lady MamaCita" Calix-Harvard Kenethia "Lady N.O. Cutie" Morgan Toya "504's Finest" Payne-Smith Akella "Baby Doll Lady 9thWD Shortie" Norton Davieione "Beauty from the East" Fairley Jessica Perrilliat Ayanna Barham Moriah Dyer Whitney Dickerson	Millisia White

NOTES

INTRODUCTION

1. Mary Ellison, "Charmaine Neville, the Mardi Gras Indians, and the Music of Opposi-tional Politics," *Popular Music and Society* 18 (1994): 19–39; George Lipsitz, "Mardi Gras Indians: Carnival and Counter-Narrative in Black New Orleans," *Cultural Critique* 10 (1988): 99–121; Maurice M. Martinez, "Delight in Repetition: The Black Indians," *Wavelength* (February 1982): 21–25; Joseph Roach, "Mardi Gras Indians and Others: Genealogies of American Performance," *Theatre Journal* 44 (1992): 461–83; Rosita M. Sands, "Carnival Celebrations in Africa and the New World: Junkanoo and the Black Indians of Mardi Gras," *Black Music Research Journal* 11 (1991): 75–92; Michael P. Smith, "Behind the Lines: The Black Mardi Gras Indians and the New Orleans Second Line," *Black Music Research Journal* 14 (1994): 43–73; Michael P. Smith, *Mardi Gras Indians* (Gretna., La: Pelican Publishing Co., 1994); and Kathryn VanSpanckeren, "The Mardi Gras Indian Song Cycle: A Heroic Tradition," *MELUS* 16 (1989–90): 41–56.

1. GENDER, RACE, AND MASKING IN THE AGE OF JIM CROW

1. Roger D. Abrahams, *Blues for New Orleans: Mardi Gras and America's Creole Soul* (Phila-delphia: University of Pennsylvania Press, 2006); Jason Berry, "African Cultural Memory in New Orleans Music," *BMR Journal* 8 (1988): 3–12; Marcia Gaudet, "'Mardi Gras, Chic-a-la-Pie': Reasserting Creole Identity through Festive Play," *Journal of American Folklore* 114 (2001): 154–74; Kevin Fox Gotham, "Marketing Mardi Gras: Commodification, Spectacle and the Political Economy of Tourism in New Orleans," *Urban Studies* 39 (2002): 1735–56; Kevin Fox Gotham, "Tourism from Above and Below: Globalization, Localization and New Orleans's Mardi Gras," *International Journal of Urban and Regional Research* 29 (2005): 309–26; James Gill, *Lords of Misrule: Mardi Gras and the Politics of Race in New Orleans* (Jackson: University Press of Mississippi, 1997); Helen A. Regis, "Second Lines, Minstrelsy, and the Contested Landscapes of New Orleans Afro-Creole Festivals," *Cultural Anthropology* 13 (1999): 472–504. For more on the role of social and pleasure clubs in Mardi Gras traditions, see chapter 4.

2. Alecia P. Long, *The Great Southern Babylon: Sex, Race, and Respectability in New Orleans, 1865–1920* (Baton Rouge: Louisiana State University Press, 2004).

3. Laurraine Goreau, *Just Mahalia, Baby: The Mahalia Jackson Story* (Gretna, La.: Pelican Publishing Co., 1984), 35.

4. In response to a statement by Dianne Rehm that "you're also perhaps going up against a huge bank of scholars who are ready to pounce on you and say, you're wrong," Schiff quipped, "Well, you're also going up against Elizabeth Taylor, which I would say is an even greater obstacle." Elizabeth Taylor is legendary for her role in the Hollywood film *Cleopatra,* which takes many liberties with the facts of the actual woman's life. For many, she has come to represent the iconic historic picture of who Cleopatra was and what she looked like. Of course, reality was much different, as Schiff learned in her research. thedianerehmshow.org/shows/2010-11-09/stacy-schiff-cleopatra/transcript, Nov 9, 2010. The emphasis on the disreputable aspects of the Baby Dolls has hidden the art form, which includes costuming, chanting, and dancing.

5. Administrative Correspondence, Saxon to Alsberg, December 6, 1935; Saxon to John P. Davis, December 16, 1935, Reel 1, Federal Writers' Project: Historic New Orleans Collection, hereafter abbreviated FWP-HNOC.

6. Lyle Saxon, Edward Dreyer, and Robert Tallant, *Gumbo Ya-Ya: Folktales of Louisiana* (Gretna, La.: Pelican Publishing Co., 2006), 1–26; Robert Tallant, *Mardi Gras . . . as It Was* (1948; Gretna, La.: Pelican Publishing Co., 1994), 230–41. All of my quotations of Beatrice Hill and other women associated with the sportin' life of the Million Dollar Baby Dolls are taken from the reports of Robert McKinney. McKinney's interviews are to be found in Robert Tallant's papers located at Northwestern State University of Louisiana's Watson Library in Natchitoches.

7. Polk's New Orleans City Directory; 1908 Orleans Parish Grooms' Marriage Index, "G through N," June 2004, files.usgwarchives.net/la/orleans/vitals/marriages/index/groom/1908mggn.txt.

8. Leland University Catalogue: Thirtieth Annual Session, n.d. books.google.com/books?id=e_sSAAAAIAAJ&q=leontine#v=snippet&q=leontine&f=false (see page 34).

9. Some of his articles for the *Chicago Defender* are: "Xavier Accepts Bid to Play Chicago Bears," December 14, 1935, national edition; "Creole Chatter," August 22, 1936, national edition; "Walter Barnes Goes to New Orleans," March 6, 1937, national edition; and "No Separation of Race at 1938 Eucharistic Congress," September 24, 1938, national edition.

10. David A. Taylor, *Soul of a People: The WPA Writers' Project Uncovers Depression America* (New York: John Wiley and Sons, 2009), 147–48.

11. *Orleans Death Indices, 1937–1948,* State of Louisiana, Secretary of State, Division of Archives, Records Management, and History (*Vital Records Indices,* Baton Rouge, LA).

12. "An Online Story of Jazz in New Orleans," Jerry Jazz Musician, www.jerryjazzmusician.com/mainHTML.cfm?page=hentoff-no-4.html (accessed July 18, 2010).

13. Mick Burns, *Keeping the Beat on the Street: The New Orleans Brass Band Renaissance* (Baton Rouge: Louisiana State University Press, 2006), 93.

14. Hollis Lynch, *The Black Urban Condition* (Ann Arbor: University of Michigan Press, 1973), 293. For more on shake dancing, as well as other characteristic forms of New Orleans dance, see chapter 2 of this book.

15. Burns, *Keeping the Beat on the Street,* 93.

16. Saxon et al., *Gumbo Ya-Ya,* 15

17. Samuel Kinser, *Carnival American Style: Mardi Gras at New Orleans and Mobile* (Chicago: University of Chicago Press, 1990), 135.

18. Eddie "Duke" Edwards, interview by the author, April 2010, Edgard, La.

19. Nickname for Storyville.

20. Ronnie Clayton, "A History of the Federal Writers' Project in Louisiana," Ph.D. diss., Louisiana State University, 1974, 253.

21. Ann Cook was born in 1886 and lived in Back o' Town. Ann sang the blues in the District in the brothel owned by Willie Piazza, a woman of color. Some women of color who were madams also played the cornet or sang opera to the accompaniment of Black male jazz legends such as Tony Jackson and Jelly Roll Morton. For more on these dual roles, see Sherrie Tucker's work on women and New Orleans jazz.

22. Danny Barker, *Buddy Bolden and the Last Days of Storyville* (Oxford, U.K.: Bayou Press, 1998).

23. Hidden History: Unknown New Orleanians, an exhibit curated by Emily Epstein Landau, mounted by the Louisiana Division, New Orleans Public Library, permanently on-line at nutrias.org/exhibits/hidden/hiddenfromhistory.htm.

24. Stephanie Stokes, "New Orleans' Iconic Street Tiles Are Falling Victim to Repair Crews," *New Orleans Times-Picayune,* June 21, 2009, blog.nola.com/news_impact/print .html?entry=/2009/06/olibbp102top2_0622aaa01_y8tile.html (accessed March 15, 2010).

25. Bureau of Identification, Department of Police, Tulane Ave. and Saratoga St., New Orleans.

26. See Keith Weldon Medley, *We as Freemen: Plessy v. Ferguson* (Gretna, La.: Pelican Publishing Co., 2003).

27. Dale A. Somers, "Black and White in New Orleans: A Study in Urban Race Relations, 1865–1900," *Journal of Southern History* 40 (1974): 19–42.

28. Ibid., 36.

29. Craig L. Foster, "Tarnished Angels: Prostitution in Storyville, New Orleans, 1900–1910," *Louisiana History* 31 (1990): 395.

30. Louis Armstrong, *Satchmo: My Life in New Orleans* (New York: Prentice-Hall, 1954), 95, 198.

31. Roger Abrahams, "Christmas and Carnival on Saint Vincent," *Western Folklore* 31 (1972): 289.

32. I have substituted the terms "black women," "black men," and "bottoms" for terms or phrases in the original that seem inappropriate to reproduce here.

33. Jason Berry, *The Spirit of Black Hawk* (Jackson: University of Mississippi Press, 1995); David C. Estes, "Across Ethnic Boundaries: St. Joseph's Day in a New Orleans Afro-American Spiritual Church," *Mississippi Folklore Register* 6 (1987): 35–43; Andrew J. Kaslow, "The Afro-American Celebration of St. Joseph's Day," in *Perspectives on Ethnicity in New Orleans,* ed. John Cook and Mackie J-V Blanton (New Orleans: Committee on Ethnicity in New Orleans, 1979), 48–52; Ethelyn G. Orso, *The St. Joseph Altar Traditions of South Louisiana* (Lafayette: University of Southwestern Louisiana, 1990); Kay Turner and Suzanne Seriff, "'Giving an Altar': The Ideology of Reproduction in a St. Joseph's Day Feast," *Journal of American Folklore* 100 (1987): 446–60.

34. Sylvester Francis, owner and curator of Backstreet Museum, suggests that the Sicilian American celebration of St. Joseph stems from the communal protection they found in his miracle. When they were hungry, embattled outcasts in their own country, St. Joseph rescued them. They return to this collective memory annually to give thanks. The Black Indians of New Orleans assert that their masking is in recognition and gratitude for the Native American people sheltering the enslaved of the region.

35. The Bernheim Bros. company had officially established the label in 1879. The initials were taken from the founder, German-born Isaac Wolfe Bernheim; "Harper" was borrowed from the name of a well-known horse breeder, F. B. Harper. The popularity of the brand could have stemmed from the awards it won at the 1885 New Orleans Exposition. (From Robin R. Preston's pre-Prohibition website for collectors of shot glasses, www.pre-pro.com/midacore/view_glass.php?sid=RRP1813.)

36. Another colorful example of liquor marketing by an African American in New Orleans was Nathan Johnny King, an employee of F. Strauss & Son, a wholesale liquor dealer. His imaginative and aggressive marketing of "Old Crow" to African Americans earned him the moniker of the "Old Crow man." See Keith Weldon Medley, *Tan Mardi Gras, Mardi Gras Guide* (Mandeville: Arthur Hardy Enterprises, 2008), 70–73.

37. This is verified by noted musicians such as George "Pops" Foster in his *Autobiography.* According to Foster, the "best whiskey was I. W. Harper, Murrayhill, and Sunnybrook." These drinks "cost ten cents in the tonks and 20 cents in the cabarets." "Long after I left New Orleans guys would come around asking me about Storyville down there. I thought it was some kind of little town we played around there that I couldn't remember. When I found out they were talking about the red-light district, I sure was surprised." Tom Stoddard and Pops Foster, *The Autobiography of Pops Foster: New Orleans Jazz Man* (Milwaukee: Hal Leonard Corp., 2005), 41.

38. Saxon et al., *Gumbo Ya-Ya,* 14. In one of the few traces of Black women speaking for themselves, we find that Black men did have an affectionate term for them, and that was "baby doll."

39. Ibid.

40. Jessica Benjamin, "An Outline of Intersubjectivity: The Development of Recognition," *Psychoanalytic Psychology* 7, supplement (1990): 33–46.

41. Judith Teicholz, "An Improvisational Attitude: Transforming Painful Patterns through Dyadic Play in Psychoanalysis," lecture, Tampa Bay Psychoanalytic Society Scientific Meeting, March 6, 2010.

2. WOMEN DANCING THE JAZZ

1. Credit goes to Eddie "Duke" Edwards for coining and promoting this expression.

2. Frank J. Gillis and John W. Miner, *Oh, Didn't He Ramble: The Life Story of Lee Collins as Told to Mary Collins* (Urbana: University of Illinois Press, 1974).

3. Robert McKinney, Federal Writers' Project (1939), Box 423, Federal Writers' Project, Cammie G. Henry Research Center, Watson Library, Northwestern State University of Louisiana.

4. Improvised, made up by the performer. Value in "hot" music is placed on playing and dancing what one feels, thinks, and experiences.

5. Danny Barker, interview by Michael White, July 21–23, 1992, Smithsonian Jazz Oral History Program, Archives Center, National Museum of American History, www.smithsonianjazz.org/oral_histories/pdf/joh_DannyBarker.pdf (accessed September 19, 2011).

6. Lawrence Gushee, "The Nineteenth-Century Origins of Jazz," *Black Music Research Journal* 14 (1994): 1–24.

7. Reid Mitchell, *All on a Mardi Gras Day: Episodes in the History of New Orleans Carnival*

(Cambridge, Mass.: Harvard University Press, 1999), 158. The tradition of the second line is discussed later in this chapter.

8. Danny Barker, *A Life in Jazz* (New York: Oxford University Press, 1986), 58.

9. To rag a tune is to enhance a single note of the melody with many dots and quicker-paced notes, which adds syncopation. A display explanation of syncopation at the Old U.S. Mint in New Orleans highlights the aim of the musical technique: "Syncopation in jazz music is what makes you want to get up and dance. Rhythmically syncopation can occur before the beat or slightly after. Syncopation adds an element of surprise by adding an accent where you wouldn't expect it."

10. Legend has it that the song "Funky Butt" originated with Buddy Bolden, who encountered a foul smell in one of the dance halls when the ventilation failed and the hall became overheated.

11. Peter Tamony, "Funky," *American Speech* 55 (1980): 210–21.

12. Marshall Stearns and Jean Stearns, *Jazz Dance: The Story of American Vernacular Dance* (New York: Macmillan Co., 1968), 21.

13. Daniel Hardie, *Exploring Early Jazz: The Origins and Evolution of the New Orleans Style* (San Jose, Calif.: Writers Club Press, 2002), 41.

14. Oscar Monte Samuels, "New Orleans Makes a Claim," *Variety,* July 1, 1911, qtd. in Gushee, "The Nineteenth-Century Origins of Jazz," 170.

15. Stearns and Stearns, *Jazz Dance,* 21.

16. Barker, *A Life in Jazz,* 77.

17. Since 2004, critical perspectives on women in jazz have been produced, including Kristin McGee's *Some Liked It Hot: Jazz Women in Film and Television, 1928–1959* (Middletown, Conn.: Wesleyan University Press, 2009).

18. Sherrie Tucker, "A Feminist Perspective on New Orleans Jazz Women," research report, New Orleans Jazz National Historical Park, 2004, 2.

19. Ibid., 11.

20. Ibid., 17.

21. Debra Mouton, personal communication, January 7, 2011.

22. The alarming rate of alcohol and drug abuse among musicians is discussed from a psychological perspective by Charles Winick. Winick listed numerous social and personal elements that led to frequent drug use by jazz musicians: many bands had several users, and there was pressure to use in order to belong; many nightclubs were hospitable to the sale of drugs; and musicians played for audiences that were in various stages of intoxication themselves and were there to have a good time. The arduous travel schedule and conditions made the musicians irritable, and they relied on drugs to "lift" them. In addition, they were able to afford drugs and had the leisure time to use them. The pleasure derived from using drugs was a frequent theme of jazz lyrics, and the lyrics also promoted a lighthearted attitude toward drug use. See Charles Winick, "How High the Moon: Jazz and Drugs," *Antioch Review* 21 (1961): 53–68. See Robert McKinney's interviews with "Baby Doll" and Beatrice Hill for his assessment of the toll drug use took on their lives.

23. Saxon et al., *Gumbo Ya-Ya,* 15

24. Sam Bonart was born in New Orleans on December 25, 1869, to immigrant parents, Hertz Bonart, from Krakow, Austria, and Bertha Cohan, from Scherwerin, Germany. S. B.

Goodkind, *Eminent Jews of America: A collection of biographical sketches of Jews who have distinguished themselves in commercial, professional and religious endeavors* (Toledo, Ohio: American Hebrew Biographical Co., 1918), 46.

25. Arthé A. Anthony, "'Lost Boundaries': Racial Passing and Poverty in Segregated New Orleans," *Louisiana History* 36 (1995): 291–312.

26. Ibid., 298.

27. Barker, *A Life in Jazz*, 69–70.

28. Daniel L. McGuire, *At the Dark End of the Street: Black Women, Rape, and Resistance: A New History of the Civil Rights Movement from Rosa Parks to the Rise of Black Power* (New York: Alfred A. Knopf, 2010).

29. LaKisha Michelle Simmons, "Black Girls Coming of Age: Sexuality and Segregation in New Orleans, 1930–1954," Ph.D. diss., University of Michigan, 2009. Also see Christina Simmons, "African Americans and Sexual Victorianism in the Social Hygiene Movement, 1910–1940," *Journal of the History of Sexuality* 4 (1993): 51–75.

30. Ibid.

31. Recent work includes Lee Sartain, *Invisible Activists: Women of the Louisiana NAACP and the Struggle for Civil Rights, 1915–1945* (Baton Rouge: Louisiana State University Press, 2007). See also Doris Dorcas Carter, "Refusing to Relinquish the Struggle: The Social Role of the Black Woman in Louisiana History," in *Louisiana's Black Heritage,* ed. R. Macdonald, J. Kemp, and E. Haas (New Orleans: Louisiana State Museum, 1979), 163–89; Arthé A. Anthony, *The Negro Creole Community in New Orleans, 1880–1920: An Oral History* (Berkeley: University of California, 1978); and Simmons, "Black Girls Coming of Age." Each author describes and analyzes Black women's lives in segregated New Orleans.

32. The double standard that values male productivity and maleness per se is captured by LaKisha Simmons. Simmons notes that Charles Guerand, the White patrolman who killed fourteen-year-old Hattie McCray because she would not allow him to rape her and who was convicted and sentenced to death, ultimately was able to avoid the death penalty by first claiming he was insane, then crossing over to sanity to stand for another trail and ultimately gain his freedom. Simmons writes that the ease with which Guerand, as a White man, was "able to cross the boundaries of insanity and sanity speaks to the way in which white men were easily brought back into the framework of New Orleans citizenship" ("Black Girls Coming of Age," 490).

33. At the beginning of the twentieth century, the "politics of respectability" was central to Black life and political thinking. According to LaKisha Simmons, those who embraced this view challenged racist views and policies, especially regarding how Black women were perceived and treated in White America. Blacks emphasized self-respect and their rights as citizens. But even Black women who adhered to the dictates of respectability could be raped with impunity by White men. Through the politics of respectability, Black women challenged their characterization as immoral, childlike, and unworthy of respect or protection ("Black Girls Coming of Age," 485).

34. Lewis A. Erenberg, "Everybody's Doin' It: The Pre–World War I Dance Craze, the Castles, and the Modern American Girl," *Feminist Studies* 3 (1975): 155–70; Julie Malnig, "Athena Meets Venus: Visions of Women in Social Dance in the Teens and Early 1920s," *Dance Research Journal* 31 (1999): 34–62.

35. Barbara S. Glass, *African American Dance: An Illustrated History* (Jefferson, N.C.: McFarland & Co., 2007), 96.

36. Rachel Shteir, *Striptease: The Untold History of the Girlie Show* (Oxford, U.K.: Oxford University Press, 2004), 88.

37. Frederic Ramsey, qtd. in Jacqui Malone, *Steppin' on the Blues: The Visible Rhythms of African American Dance* (Urbana: University of Illinois Press, 1996), 140.

38. Stearns and Stearns, *Jazz Dance,* 18.

39. S. Smith, "Muntu Troupe: A Jazzy, Riotous Extravaganza," *Chicago Tribune,* April 11, 1998, articles.chicagotribune.com/1998-04-11/news/9804110120_1_mardi-gras-dances-fat (accessed June 12, 2011).

40. Some Negro Customs, Folder 33, Federal Writers' Project, Cammie G. Henry Research Center, Watson Library, Northwestern State University of Louisiana.

41. Lyle Saxon, *Fabulous New Orleans* (Gretna, La.: Pelican Publishing Co., 1988), 48.

42. Ibid., 49.

43. Andrew Justin, "The Wild Tremé Mardi Gras Indians." http://wildtreme.com/The_History.html (accessed August 25, 2012).

44. Interview with Andrew Justin, January 31, 2012.

45. Joseph Lee, "Play as an Antidote to Civilization," *Playground* 5 (1911): 125.

46. People in New Orleans are masters of the moniker. Danny Barker explained to his interviewer that older people would give a baby a nickname based on an essential but humorous characteristic of that child, and it would stick.

47. Erenberg, "Everybody's Doin' It," 165.

3. "OH YOU BEAUTIFUL DOLL"

1. "Williams's song 'You're Some Pretty Doll' (1917) had already been performed by the Ziegfeld Follies, sold to Shapiro and Bernstein for publication, and recorded for Columbia by Samuel Ashe," according to Anne Key Simpson in "Those Everlasting Blues: The Best of Clarence Williams," *Louisiana History* 40 (Spring 1999): 186.

2. Jelly Roll Morton, *A Fragment of an Autobiography,* 1944, www.doctorjazz.co.uk/fragment.html (accessed July 18, 2010).

3. Philip W. Scher, "Copyright Heritage: Preservation, Carnival, and the State in Trinidad," *Anthropological Quarterly* 75 (2002): 453–84.

4. *Jamette* refers to a working-class woman who masked at Carnival and eschewed proper Victorian decorum. These women dressed in provocative costumes, confronted White and Black men, demanded money, fought, sang, and drank as far back as the nineteenth century in Trinidad's carnivals. Dylan Kerrigan, "Creatures of the Mas," *Caribbean Beat* 71 (January–February 2005): www.meppublishers.com/online/caribbean-beat/archive/index.php?id=cb71-1-38&print=1 (accessed September 24, 2011).

5. Samantha A. Noel, "*De Jamette in We:* Redefining Performance in Contemporary Trinidad Carnival," *Small Axe* 14 (2010): 60–78.

6. Qtd. in Kerrigan, "Creatures of the Mas."

7. Ragan Wicker, "Nineteenth-Century New Orleans and a Carnival of Women," M.A. thesis, University of Florida, 2006.

8. Robin Roberts, "New Orleans Mardi Gras and Gender in Three Krewes: Rex, The Truck Parades, and Muses," *Western Folklore* 65 (2006): 303–28.

9. *Tableau* designates the theme of a float or a theme or several themes of the ball.

10. Roberts, "New Orleans Mardi Gras and Gender in Three Krewes."

11. Robert McKinney, "Queen Catherine Riley Talks, at Last!" FWP Folder (n.d.): 582. Leopold LeBlanc was king.

12. The official location of City Hall.

13. Robert McKinney and Hazel Breaux Odette Delillie (Negro), FWP Folder 56 (February 13, 1939). Allen James was king.

14. Robert Tallant, "Negroes in the Carnival," FWP Folder 434 (n.d.). Emanuel Bernard was king. Odette offered that the king was respectful to her and never approached her in an untoward manner. This is in distinction to Catherine Riley and Ceola Carter, through their admission, and the rumor mill seemed to indicate an intimate connection to the Zulu club officials.

15. Belinda Edmondson, "Public Spectacles: Caribbean Women and the Politics of Public Performance," *Small Axe* 7 (2003): 1–16.

16. Sarah Carpenter, "Women and Carnival Masking," *Records of Early English Drama Newsletter* 21 (1996): 9–16.

17. Ken Plummer, "The Sexual Spectacle: Making a Public Culture of Sexual Problems," in *Handbook of Social Problems: A Comparative International Perspective,* ed. George Ritzer (Thousand Oaks, Calif.: Sage Publications, 2004), 521–41. The public education function of Carnival is not lost on Shalini Puri, who writes that "it is further possible that carnival trains the public in a politics of irony in which radical knowledge may be yoked to conservative action" ("Beyond Resistance: Notes toward a New Caribbean Cultural Studies," *Small Axe* 7 [2003]: 27).

18. Plummer, "The Sexual Spectacle," 530.

19. Pamela R. Franco, "'Dressing Up and Looking Good': Afro-Creole Female Maskers in Trinidad Carnival," *African Arts* 31 (1998): 62–67, 91, 95–96.

20. Edmondson, "Public Spectacles," 5.

21. Pamela R. Franco, "The 'Unruly Woman' in Nineteenth-Century Trinidad Carnival," *Small Axe* 7 (2000): 60–77.

22. Franco, "'Dressing Up and Looking Good,'" 76.

23. Noel, *"De Jamette in We,"* 63.

24. Ibid., 61.

25. Edmondson, "Public Spectacles," 3.

26. Carpenter, "Women and Carnival Masking."

27. Franco, "'Dressing Up and Looking Good,'" 63.

28. Trinna S. Frever, "'Oh! You Beautiful Doll!': Icon, Image, and Culture in Works by Alvarez, Cisneros, and Morrison," *Tulsa Studies in Women's Literature* 28 (2009): 122.

29. Ibid., 123.

30. Ibid., 124.

31. Alan Lomax, *Mister Jelly Roll: The Fortunes of Jelly Roll Morton, New Orleans Creole and "Inventor of Jazz"* (1950; rpt. Berkeley: University of California Press, 1993), 49.

32. Sidney Bechet (May 14, 1897–May 14, 1959) was born in the early years of Storyville and

lived through the heyday of the Mardi Gras Baby Dolls. Sidney Bechet and Rudi Blesh, *Treat It Gentle: An Autobiography* (New York: Da Capo Press, 2002), 82.

33. Gerilyn G. Tandberg, "Sinning for Silk: Dress-for-Success Fashions of the New Orleans Storyville Prostitute," *Women's Studies International Forum* 13 (1990): 229–48. "An example of it may be seen in the Figure 6 illustration of an 1898 advertisement for a Mardi Gras ball found in the *Blue Book (1898)*. Figure 7 records Ernest Bellocq's photograph of a prostitute wearing one."

34. Ibid., 237.

35. Ibid., 242.

36. Ibid., 240.

37. Ibid.

38. Long, *The Great Southern Babylon*.

39. Robert McKinney, "A Real Baby Doll Speaks Her Mind," FWP Folder 423 (February 9, 1940).

40. Interview with Mary Davis at the Suzy Q Barroom at South Rampart and Thalia streets, December 23, 1938.

41. McKinney, "A Real Baby Doll Speaks Her Mind."

42. See Monique Guillory, "Under One Roof: Sins and Sanctity of the New Quadroon Balls," in *Race Consciousness: African-American Studies for the New Century*, ed. Judith Jackson Fossett and Jeffrey A. Tucker (New York: New York University Press, 1997), 65–92.

43. Laura Mulvey, "Visual Pleasure and Narrative Cinema," *Screen* 16 (1975): 6–18.

44. One example is Al Rose, *Storyville, New Orleans: Being an Authentic, Illustrated Account of the Notorious Red-Light District* (Tuscaloosa: University of Alabama Press, 1974).

45. Personal communication, April 14, 2011.

46. Ibid., March 26, 2011.

47. U.S. Census 1920, Louisiana, Orleans Parish, New Orleans, 3rd Ward, SD1 ED34, Sheet 14B, line 72, at 539 Franklin Street.

48. U.S. Census 1910, Louisiana, Orleans Parish, New Orleans, 3rd Ward, SD1 ED31, Sheet 22B, line 57, at 524 Franklin Street.

49. U.S. Census 1930, Louisiana, Orleans Parish, New Orleans, 3rd Ward, SD11 ED36–42, Sheet 14B, line 66, at 539 Loyola Avenue (was Franklin in the 1920 census).

50. U.S. Census 1930, Louisiana, Orleans Parish, New Orleans, 3rd Ward, SD11 ED36–42, Sheet 11A, line 1, at 454 S. Liberty Street.

51. Barker, interview.

52. Barbara Smith Corrales, "Prurience, Prostitution, and Progressive Improvements: The Crowley Connection, 1909–1918," *Louisiana History* 45 (2004): 37–70.

53. "Landau, Emily. (2011, May 8). Storyville." Retrieved May 8, 2011, from KnowLA Encyclopedia of Louisiana: www.www.knowla.org/entry.php?rec=739

54. L'Hote v. City of New Orleans, 177 U.S. 587 (1900).

55. City of New Orleans v. Willie V. Piazza v., No. 22,624, 1917. See also Long, *The Great Southern Babylon*.

56. Shirley J. Carlson, "Black Ideals of Womanhood in the Late Victorian Era," *Journal of Negro History* 77 (1992): 61–73.

57. Elizabeth J. Stigler makes the case for gender outlaws or transwomen who participated

in roller derby in "Trans on the Track: Policing of Gender in the All-Women Space of Flat Track Roller Derby" (presentation, Florida Consortium for Women's and Gender Studies, Boca Raton, April 1–2, 2011).

58. Ibid.

59. Jeff Nall, "Reproduction of the Patriarchal Feminine Ideal (Emphasized Femininity) in Cultural Representations of Childbirth" (presentation, Florida Consortium for Women's and Gender Studies, Boca Raton, April 1–2, 2011).

60. Barker, interview.

61. Sterling Brown, "Negro Folk Expression: Spirituals, Seculars, Ballads, and Work Songs," *Phylon* 14 (1953): 45–61.

62. Berry, "African Cultural Memory in New Orleans Music," 8.

63. VanSpanckeren, "The Mardi Gras Indian Song Cycle," 41–48.

64. Berry, *The Spirit of Black Hawk,* 8.

65. The middle passage was the longest part of the trip made by slave ships, the part of the Atlantic Ocean between the west coast of Africa and the West Indies. Irene Diggs, "Singing and Dancing in Afro Cuba," *The Crisis* 58 (Dec. 1951): 663.

66. Paula J. Gidding, *When and Where I Enter: The Impact of Black Women on Race and Sex in America* (New York: Harper, 2001).

67. Diggs, "Singing and Dancing in Afro Cuba," 161.

68. Leonard V. Huber, *Mardi Gras: A Pictorial History of Carnival in New Orleans* (Gretna, La.: Pelican Publishing Co., 1976), 69.

69. Ronnie W. Clayton, "The Federal Writers' Project for Blacks in Louisiana," *Louisiana History* 19 (1978): 327–35.

70. Ibid., 330. "Blacks, in general, were more expressive to the Dillard writers than they were to the white writers of the Louisiana Writers' Project," a conclusion Clayton derived from his interview with Caroline Durieux, January 27, 1974.

71. Robert McKinney, "Captain Jackson Keeps the Baby Dolls from Strutting their Stuff: Indians Come Out," FWP Folder 423 (March 19, 1940): 3.

72. Donald Bogle, *Toms, Coons, Mulattoes, Mammies, and Bucks: An Interpretive History of Blacks in American Films* (New York: Continuum International Publishing Group, 2001), xii.

73. Ibid., xxi.

74. Ibid., xxii.

75. McKinney, FWP Folder 423.

76. Lawrence W. Levine, *Black Culture and Black Consciousness: Afro-American Folk Thought from Slavery to Freedom* (Oxford, U.K.: Oxford University Press, 1978), 300.

77. Beatrice Hill, told to Robert McKinney, March 11, 12, 14, 1940.

78. The song "When the Saints Go Marching In" is critiqued by Ralph Slovenko as being misrepresented when characterized as religious only. Slovenko's experience as a native New Orleanian led him to conclude that the song, when sung in the brothels, pokes fun at the "upstanding, business, and family men who frequented the District's brothels" ("When the Saints Go Marching In," *Journal of Psychiatry and Law* 28 [2000]: 553–64).

79. Count Basie arranged and performed a version of "Momma Don't Wear No Drawers." The Million Dollar Baby Dolls added much profanity to the lyrics.

80. Kim Marie Vaz, "Teacher Helps Students Get a Head Start," *New Orleans Times Pica-*

yune, July 13, 1989, www.canerivercolony.com/CreoleHistory/CreoleHistory.htm#martinez (accessed October 15, 2011).

81. Martinez has produced other films exploring the African American experience in New Orleans: *Too White to Be Black and Too Black to Be White: The New Orleans Creoles* and *Wings of Wood: The Art of Creole Wood Carvers of New Orleans.*

82. Martinez could not recall the spelling of this last name.

83. Johnny Heckman's shoe store near the St. Bernard market on the corner going toward LaHarpe Street sold a lot of Carnival materials, including trim and satin, but they were known for shoes, the black patent-leather ones with the strap across.

84. Interview with author, June 24, 2011.

4. A NEW GROUP OF BABY DOLLS HITS THE STREETS

1. Mitchell, *All on a Mardi Gras Day.*

2. Guillory, "Under One Roof."

3. Carolyn Ware, "Anything to Act Crazy: Cajun Women and Mardi Gras Disguise," *Journal of American Folklore* 114 (2001): 240.

4. Karen Trahan Leathem, "A Carnival According to Their Own Desire: Gender and Mardi Gras in New Orleans, 1870–1910," Ph.D. diss., University of North Carolina, 1994.

5. Tallant, *Mardi Gras . . . as It Was,* 127.

6. Leathem, "A Carnival According to Their Own Desire," 200.

7. Ibid., 232.

8. Ibid., 224

9. Tallant, *Mardi Gras . . . as It Was,* 239–41.

10. Maurice M. Martinez, "A Conversation on Artist John McCrady," *Xavier Review* 13 (1993): 2.

11. Ralph L. Wickiser, Caroline Durieux, and John McCrady, *Mardi Gras Day* (New York: Henry Holt, 1948), 16–17.

12. "Shotgun" refers to an architectural style. This wooden structure is narrow with all the rooms lined up in a row. A hallway travels from the front of the house to the rear. The houses are erected on raised brick piers with a small porch, a roof apron, and Victorian lace ornamentation.

13. The seventeenth-century French playwright, satirized because of the shape of his nose.

14. Wickiser et al., *Mardi Gras Day,* 6–7.

15. Blake Woods, personal communication, October 31, 2011.

16. R. McKinney, "History of the Baby Dolls," 1939, Folder 423, Federal Writers' Project, Cammie G. Henry Research Center, Watson Library, Northwestern State University of Louisiana.

17. Tucker, "A Feminist Perspective on New Orleans Jazz Women," 16.

18. Jeff Hannusch, "The South's Swankiest Night Spot: The Legend of the Dew Drop Inn" (1997), www.satchmo.com/ikoiko/dewdropinn.html.

19. The Baby Dolls and Gold Diggers were seen by outside observers as a largely working-class female performative tradition as late as the 1950s. See Munro S. Edmonson, "Carnival in New Orleans," *Caribbean Quarterly* 4 (1956): 233–45.

20. Interview with Kenneth Leslie, August 8, 2010.

21. Burns, *Keeping the Beat on the Street*, 101.

22. Jonathon Green, *Cassell's Dictionary of Slang* (New York: Sterling Publishing Co., 2005).

23. Marybeth Hamilton, "Sexual Politics and African-American Music; or, Placing Little Richard in History," *History Workshop Journal* 46 (1998): 160–76.

24. Thaddeus Russell, "The Color of Discipline: Civil Rights and Black Sexuality," *American Quarterly* 60 (2008): 101–28.

25. Kalamu ya Salaam, "New Orleans Mardi Gras Indians and Tootie Montana," (1997), www.louisianafolklife.org/LT/Virtual_Books/Hes_Prettiest/hes_the_prettiest_tootie_montana.html (accessed June 12, 2011).

26. VanSpanckeren, "The Mardi Gras Indian Song Cycle," 44.

27. Ibid., 53.

28. Regis, "Second Lines, Minstrelsy, and the Contested Landscapes of New Orleans Afro-Creole Festivals," 472–504.

29. Ibid., 473.

30. Interview with Mercedes Stevenson, March 26, 2011.

31. Circa late 1930s, early 1940s, Twelfth Ward Baby Dolls.

32. Given the relationship between social and pleasure clubs and local Black businesses, Alma Batiste's group may have received sponsorship from a local club in town at that time called the Golden Slipper.

33. Jerry Brock, "The Million Dollar Baby Dolls," *New Orleans Beat Street Magazine* 2 (2004): 7–8.

34. Barker, interview.

35. H. Brook Webb, "The Slang of Jazz," *American Speech* 12 (1937): 179–84.

36. McKinney, "A Real Baby Doll Speaks Her Mind," 3.

37. Michael Proctor Smith, *A Joyful Noise: A Celebration of New Orleans Music* (Gretna, La.: Pelican Publishing Co., 1990), 61.

38. "Black Astrologers Predict the Future," *Ebony* (April 1969): 60–79. Much of the information in this paragraph came from a personal communication with Elaine Gutierrez, April 5, 2012.

39. Interview by Kim Vaz and Millisia White, April 25, 2010.

5. "WE ARE NO GENERATION"

1. See Charles Chamberlain, "The Goodson Sisters: Women Pianists and the Function of Gender in the Jazz Age," *Jazz Archivist* 15 (2001): 8; and Tucker, "A Feminist Perspective on New Orleans Jazz Women," 199.

2. Tallant, *Mardi Gras . . . as It Was*, 109.

3. Rick McRae, "'What Is Hip?' and Other Inquiries in Jazz Slang Lexicography," *Notes* 57 (2001): 574–84.

4. Vincent J. Panetta, "'For Godsake Stop!' Improvised Music in the Streets of New Orleans, ca. 1890," *Musical Quarterly* 84 (2000): 5–29.

5. Terry Monaghan, "Why Study the Lindy Hop?" *Dance Research Journal* 33 (2001): 124–27.

6. Scott DeVeaux, "The Emergence of the Jazz Concert, 1935–1945," *American Music* 7 (1989): 6–29.

7. Rhonda McKendall, "Remember When? Carnival on Claiborne Is Relived," *New Orleans States-Item,* February 1, 1978, B-10.

8. Tallant, "Negroes in the Carnival."

9. Interview with Resa (Cinnamon Black) Wilson-Bazile, January 2011 (about the 1970s era).

10. Interview with Miriam Batiste Reed, April 22, 2010, Millisia White co-interviewer, and interview with Eva Perry and Geanie Thomas, April 25, 2010.

11. Interview with Resa (Cinnamon Black) Wilson-Bazile, January 2011.

12. Katrina Hazzard-Gordon, "Afro-American Core Culture Social Dance: An Examination of Four Aspects of Meaning," *Dance Research Journal* 15 (1983): 21–26.

13. Noah Bonaparte Pais, "Rally of the Dolls," *Gambit,* February 16, 2009, www.bestofneworleans.com/gyrobase/rally-of-the-dolls/Content?oid=1256917&mode=print.

14. Interview with Deja Andrews, April 25, 2010.

15. Photos of Antoinette K-Doe, Miriam Reed, Geannie Thomas, and Eva Perry at this event can be found in Angelo and Peter Coclanis, "Jazz Funeral: A Living Tradition," *Southern Cultures* 11 (2005): 86–92.

16. Geannie Thomas (an Ernie K-Doe Baby Doll), interview by Kim Vaz and Millisia White, April 25, 2010.

17. Interview with Millisia White (founder, New Orleans Society of Dance's Baby Doll Ladies, and "Lady Bee"), April 22, 2010.

18. Ibid.

19. Lois Nelson, Merline Kimble, and Patricia McDonald, interview by Kim Vaz and Millisia White, April 25, 2010.

20. Helen A. Regis, "Blackness and the Politics of Memory in the New Orleans Second Line," *American Ethnologist* 28 (2001): 752–77.

21. Interview with Kenethia "Lady N.O. Cutie" Morgan, April 24, 2010, New Orleans Society of Dance's Baby Doll Ladies.

22. Davieione (Beauty from the East) Fairley, April 24, 2010, New Orleans Society of Dance's Baby Doll Ladies.

BIBLIOGraPHY

Abrahams, Roger D. *Blues for New Orleans: Mardi Gras and America's Creole Soul.* Philadelphia: University of Pennsylvania Press, 2006.

———. "Christmas and Carnival on Saint Vincent." *Western Folklore* 31 (1972): 275–89.

Anthony, Arthé A. "'Lost Boundaries': Racial Passing and Poverty in Segregated New Orleans." *Louisiana History* 36 (1995): 291–312.

———. *The Negro Creole Community in New Orleans, 1880–1920: An Oral History.* Berkeley: University of California, 1978.

Balme, Christopher B. "Sexual Spectacles: Theatricality and the Performance of Sex in Early Encounters in the Pacific." *TDR* 44 (2000): 67–85.

Barker, Danny. *Buddy Bolden and the Last Days of Storyville.* Oxford, U.K.: Bayou Press, 1998.

———. *A Life in Jazz.* Edited by Alyn Shipton. New York: Oxford University Press, 1986.

Barnes, Natasha. "Body Talk: Notes on Women and Spectacle in Contemporary Trinidad Carnival." *Small Axe* 7 (2000): 93–105.

Bechet, Sidney, and Rudi Blesh. *Treat It Gentle: An Autobiography.* New York: Da Capo Press, 2002.

Benjamin, Jessica. "An Outline of Intersubjectivity: The Development of Recognition." *Psychoanalytic Psychology* 7, supplement (1990): 33–46.

Berry, Jason. "African Cultural Memory in New Orleans Music." *BMR Journal* 8 (1988): 3–12.

———. *The Spirit of Black Hawk: A Mystery of Africans and Indians.* Jackson: University Press of Mississippi, 1995.

Brock, Jerry. "The Million Dollar Baby Dolls." *New Orleans Beat Street Magazine* 2 (2004): 7–8.

Brown, Sterling. "Negro Folk Expression: Spirituals, Seculars, Ballads, and Work Songs." *Phylon* 14 (1953): 45–61.

Burns, Mick. *Keeping the Beat on the Street: The New Orleans Brass Band Renaissance.* Baton Rouge: Louisiana State University Press, 2008.

Carlson, Shirley J. "Black Ideals of Womanhood in the Late Victorian Era." *Journal of Negro History* 77 (1992): 61–73.

Carpenter, Sarah. "Women and Carnival Masking." *Records of Early English Drama Newsletter* 21 (1996): 9–16.

Carter, Doris Dorcas. "Refusing to Relinquish the Struggle: The Social Role of the Black Woman in Louisiana History." In *Louisiana's Black Heritage,* ed. Robert R. Macdonald, John R. Kemp, and Edward F. Haas. New Orleans: Louisiana State Museum, 1979. 163–89.

Chamberlain, Charles. "The Goodson Sisters: Women Pianists and the Function of Gender in the Jazz Age." *Jazz Archivist* 15 (2001): 8.

Clayton, Ronnie W. "The Federal Writers' Project for Blacks in Louisiana." *Louisiana History* 19 (1978): 327–35.

Coclanis, Angelo, and Peter Coclanis. "Jazz Funeral: A Living Tradition." *Southern Cultures* 11 (2005): 86–92.

Corrales, Barbara Smith. "Prurience, Prostitution, and Progressive Improvements: The Crowley Connection, 1909–1918." *Louisiana History* 45 (2004): 37–70.

DeVeaux, Scott. "The Emergence of the Jazz Concert, 1935–1945." *American Music* 7 (1989): 6–29.

Diggs, Irene. "Singing and Dancing in Afro Cuba." *The Crisis* 58 (Dec. 1951): 661–64.

Edmondson, Belinda. "Public Spectacles: Caribbean Women and the Politics of Public Performance." *Small Axe* 7 (2003): 1–16.

Ellison, Mary. "Charmaine Neville, the Mardi Gras Indians, and the Music of Oppositional Politics." *Popular Music and Society* 18 (1994): 19–39.

Erenberg, Lewis A. "Everybody's Doin' It: The Pre–World War I Dance Craze, the Castles, and the Modern American Girl." *Feminist Studies* 3 (1975): 155–70.

Estes, David C. "Across Ethnic Boundaries: St. Joseph's Day in a New Orleans Afro-American Spiritual Church." *Mississippi Folklore Register* 6 (1987): 35–43.

Foster, Craig L. "Tarnished Angels: Prostitution in Storyville, New Orleans, 1900–1910." *Louisiana History* 31 (1990): 387–97.

Franco, Pamela R. "'Dressing Up and Looking Good': Afro-Creole Female Maskers in Trinidad Carnival." *African Arts* 31 (1998): 62–67, 91, 95–96.

———. "The 'Unruly Woman' in Nineteenth-Century Trinidad Carnival." *Small Axe* 7 (2000): 60–77.

Frever, Trinna S. "'Oh! You Beautiful Doll!': Icon, Image, and Culture in Works by Alvarez, Cisneros, and Morrison." *Tulsa Studies in Women's Literature* 28 (2009): 121–39.

Gaudet, Marcia. "'Mardi Gras, Chic-a-la-Pie': Reasserting Creole Identity through Festive Play." *Journal of American Folklore* 114 (2001): 154–74.

Gill, James. *Lords of Misrule: Mardi Gras and the Politics of Race in New Orleans.* Jackson: University Press of Mississippi, 1997.

Gillis, Frank J., and John W. Miner, eds. *Oh, Didn't He Ramble: The Life Story of Lee*

Collins as Told to Mary Collins. Urbana: University of Illinois Press, 1974.

Glass, Barbara S. *African American Dance: An Illustrated History.* Jefferson, N.C.: Mc-Farland & Co., 2006.

Goodkind, S. B. *Eminent Jews of America: A collection of biographical sketches of Jews who have distinguished themselves in commercial, professional and religious endeavors.* Toledo, Ohio: American Hebrew Biographical Co., 1918.

Goreau, Laurraine. *Just Mahalia, Baby: The Mahalia Jackson Story.* Gretna, La.: Pelican Publishing Co., 1984.

Gotham, Kevin Fox. "Marketing Mardi Gras: Commodification, Spectacle, and the Political Economy of Tourism in New Orleans." *Urban Studies* 39 (2002): 1735–56.

———. "Tourism from Above and Below: Globalization, Localization, and New Orleans's Mardi Gras." *International Journal of Urban and Regional Research* 29 (2005): 309–26.

Green, Jonathon. *Cassell's Dictionary of Slang.* New York: Sterling Publishing Co., 2005.

Guillory, Monique. "Under One Roof: Sins and Sanctity of the New Quadroon Balls." In *Race Consciousness: African-American Studies for the New Century,* ed. Judith Jackson Fossett and Jeffrey A. Tucker. New York: New York University Press, 1997. 65–92.

Gushee, Lawrence. "The Nineteenth-Century Origins of Jazz." *Black Music Research Journal* 14 (1994): 1–24.

Hamilton, Marybeth. "Sexual Politics and African-American Music; or, Placing Little Richard in History." *History Workshop Journal* 46 (1998): 160–76.

Hannusch, Jeff. "The South's Swankiest Night Spot: The Legend of the Dew Drop Inn." 1997. www.satchmo.com/ikoiko/dewdropinn.html.

Hardie, Daniel. *Exploring Early Jazz: The Origins and Evolution of the New Orleans Style.* San Jose, Calif.: Writers Club Press, 2002.

Hazzard-Gordon, Katrina. "Afro-American Core Culture Social Dance: An Examination of Four Aspects of Meaning." *Dance Research Journal* 15 (1983): 21–26.

Jackson, Peter. "Street Life: The Politics of Carnival." *Environment and Planning D: Society and Space* 6 (1988): 213–27.

Kane, Harnett Thomas. *Queen New Orleans: City by the River.* New York: W. Morrow, 1949.

Kaslow, Andrew J. "The Afro-American Celebration of St. Joseph's Day." In *Perspectives on Ethnicity in New Orleans,* ed. John Cook and Mackie J-V Blanton. New Orleans: Committee on Ethnicity in New Orleans, 1979. 48–52.

Kerrigan, Dylan. "Creatures of the Mas." *Caribbean Beat* 71 (January–February 2005): www.meppublishers.com/online/caribbean-beat/archive/index.php?id=cb71-1-38&print=1 (accessed September 24, 2011).

Kinser, Samuel. *Carnival American Style: Mardi Gras in New Orleans and Mobile.* Chicago: University of Chicago Press, 1990.

Leathem, Karen Trahan. "A Carnival According to Their Own Desires: Gender and Mardi Gras in New Orleans, 1870-1910." PhD diss., University of North Carolina, 1994.

Lee, Joseph. "Play as an Antidote to Civilization." *Playground* 5 (1911): 110-26.

Levine, Lawrence W. *Black Culture and Black Consciousness: Afro-American Folk Thought from Slavery to Freedom.* Oxford, U.K.: Oxford University Press, 1978.

Lipsitz, George. "Mardi Gras Indians: Carnival and Counter-Narrative in Black New Orleans." *Cultural Critique* 10 (1988): 99-121.

Lomax, Alan. *Mister Jelly Roll: The Fortunes of Jelly Roll Morton, New Orleans Creole and "Inventor of Jazz."* 1950. Rpt. Berkeley: University of California Press, 1993.

Long, Alecia P. *The Great Southern Babylon: Sex, Race, and Respectability in New Orleans, 1865-1920.* Baton Rouge: Louisiana State University Press, 2005.

Lynch, Hollis. *The Black Urban Condition.* Ann Arbor: University of Michigan Press, 1973.

Malnig, Julie. "Athena Meets Venus: Visions of Women in Social Dance in the Teens and Early 1920s." *Dance Research Journal* 31 (1999): 34-62.

Malone, Jacqui. *Steppin' on the Blues: The Visible Rhythms of African American Dance.* Urbana: University of Illinois Press, 1996.

Martinez, Maurice M. "A Conversation on Artist John McCrady." *Xavier Review* 13 (1993): 1-14.

———. "Delight in Repetition: The Black Indians." *Wavelength* (February 1982): 21-25.

McGee, Kristin A. *Some Liked It Hot: Jazz Women in Film and Television, 1928-1959.* Middletown, Conn.: Wesleyan University Press, 2009.

McGuire, Daniel L. *At the Dark End of the Street: Black Women, Rape, and Resistance: A New History of the Civil Rights Movement from Rosa Parks to the Rise of Black Power.* New York: Alfred A. Knopf, 2010.

McRae, Rick. "'What Is Hip?' and Other Inquiries in Jazz Slang Lexicography." *Notes* 57 (2001): 574-84.

Medley, Keith Weldon. *Tan Mardi Gras: Mardi Gras Guide.* Mandeville, La.: Arthur Hardy Enterprises, 2008. 70-73.

———. *We as Freemen: Plessy v. Ferguson.* Gretna, La.: Pelican Publishing Co., 2003.

Mitchell, Reid. *All on a Mardi Gras Day: Episodes in the History of New Orleans Carnival.* Cambridge, Mass.: Harvard University Press, 1999.

——— "Carnival and Katrina." *Journal of American History* 94 (2007): 789-94.

Monaghan, Terry. "Why Study the Lindy Hop?" *Dance Research Journal* 33 (2001): 124-27.

Morton, Jelly Roll [Ferdinand Joseph LaMothe]. *A Fragment of an Autobiography.* 1944. www.doctorjazz.co.uk/fragment.html (accessed July 18, 2010).

Mulvey, Laura. "Visual Pleasure and Narrative Cinema." *Screen* 16 (1975): 6-18.

Nall, Jeff. "Reproduction of the Patriarchal Feminine Ideal (Emphasized Femininity) in Cultural Representations of Childbirth." Presentation, Florida Consortium for Women's and Gender Studies, Boca Raton, April 1–2, 2011.

Noel, Samantha A. "*De Jamette in We:* Redefining Performance in Contemporary Trinidad Carnival." *Small Axe* 14 (2010): 60–78.

Oliver, Paul. *Conversation with the Blues.* Oxford: Cambridge University Press, 1997.

Orso, Ethelyn G. *The St. Joseph Altar Traditions of South Louisiana.* Lafayette: University of Southwestern Louisiana, 1990.

Panetta, Vincent J. "'For Godsake Stop!' Improvised Music in the Streets of New Orleans, ca. 1890." *Musical Quarterly* 84 (2000): 5–29.

Pinto, Samantha. "'Why Must All Girls Want to be Flag Women?': Postcolonial Sexualities, National Reception, and Caribbean Soca Performance." *Meridians* 10 (2009): 137–63.

Plummer, Ken. "The Sexual Spectacle: Making a Public Culture of Sexual Problems." In *Handbook of Social Problems: A Comparative International Perspective,* ed. George Ritzer. Thousand Oaks, Calif.: Sage Publications, 2004. 521–41.

Puri, Shalini. "Beyond Resistance: Notes toward a New Caribbean Cultural Studies." *Small Axe* 7 (2003): 23–38.

Regis, Helen A. "Blackness and the Politics of Memory in the New Orleans Second Line." *American Ethnologist* 28 (2001): 752–77.

———. "Second Lines, Minstrelsy, and the Contested Landscapes of New Orleans Afro-Creole Festivals." *Cultural Anthropology* 13 (1999): 472–504.

Roach, Joseph. "Carnival and the Law in New Orleans." *TDR* 37 (1993): 42–75.

———. "Mardi Gras Indians and Others: Genealogies of American Performance." *Theatre Journal* 44 (1992): 461–83.

Roberts, Robin. "New Orleans Mardi Gras and Gender in Three Krewes: Rex, the Truck Parades, and Muses." *Western Folklore* 65 (2006): 303–28.

Rose, Al. *Storyville, New Orleans: Being an Authentic, Illustrated Account of the Notorious Red-Light District.* Tuscaloosa: University of Alabama Press, 1974.

Russell, Thaddeus. "The Color of Discipline: Civil Rights and Black Sexuality." *American Quarterly* 60 (2008): 101–28.

Russell, William. "Jazz Sources." *Dance Observer* 7 (1940): 140–41, 144.

Russo, Mary. "Female Grotesques: Carnival and Theory." In *Feminist Studies/Critical Studies,* ed. Teresa de Laurentis. Bloomington: Indiana University Press, 1986.

Salaam, Kalamu ya. "New Orleans Mardi Gras Indians and Tootie Montana." 1997. www.louisianafolklife.org/LT/Virtual_Books/Hes_Prettiest/hes_the_prettiest_tootie_montana.html (accessed June 12, 2011).

Sands, Rosita M. "Carnival Celebrations in Africa and the New World: Junkanoo and the Black Indians of Mardi Gras." *Black Music Research Journal* 11 (1991): 75–92.

Sartain, Lee. *Invisible Activists: Women of the Louisiana NAACP and the Struggle for Civil Rights, 1915–1945.* Baton Rouge: Louisiana State University Press, 2007.

Saxon, Lyle. *Fabulous New Orleans.* Gretna, La.: Pelican Publishing Co., 1988.

Saxon, Lyle, Edward Dreyer, and Robert Tallant. *Gumbo Ya-Ya: Folktales of Louisiana.* 1945. Gretna, La.: Pelican Publishing Co., 2006.

Scher, Philip W. "Copyright Heritage: Preservation, Carnival, and the State in Trinidad." *Anthropological Quarterly* 75 (2002): 453–84.

Schindler, Henri. *Mardi Gras: New Orleans.* Paris: Flammarion, 1997.

Shrum, Wesley, and John Kilburn. "Ritual Disrobement at Mardi Gras: Ceremonial Exchange and Moral Order." *Social Forces* 75 (1996): 423–25.

Shteir, Rachel. *Striptease: The Untold History of the Girlie Show.* Oxford, U.K.: Oxford University Press, 2004.

Simmons, Christina. "African Americans and Sexual Victorianism in the Social Hygiene Movement, 1910–1940." *Journal of the History of Sexuality* 4 (1993): 51–75.

Simmons, LaKisha Michelle. "Black Girls Coming of Age: Sexuality and Segregation in New Orleans, 1930–1954." Ph.D. diss., University of Michigan, 2009.

Simpson, Anne Key. "Those Everlasting Blues: The Best of Clarence Williams." *Louisiana History* 40 (Spring 1999): 179–95.

Slovenko, Ralph. "When the Saints Go Marching In." *Journal of Psychiatry and Law* 28 (2000): 553–64.

Smith, Michael P. "Behind the Lines: The Black Mardi Gras Indians and the New Orleans Second Line." *Black Music Research Journal* 14 (1994): 43–73.

———. *Mardi Gras Indians.* Gretna, La.: Pelican Publishing Co., 1994.

Smith-Rosenberg, Carroll. *Disorderly Conduct: Visions of Gender in Victorian America.* New York: Alfred A. Knopf, 1985.

Somers, Dale A. "Black and White in New Orleans: A Study in Urban Race Relations, 1865–1900." *Journal of Southern History* 40 (1974): 19–42.

Stearns, Marshall, and Jean Stearns. *Jazz Dance: The Story of American Vernacular Dance.* New York: Macmillan Co., 1968.

Steele, Valerie. *Fashion and Eroticism: Ideals of Feminine Beauty from the Victorian Era to the Jazz Age.* New York: Oxford University Press, 1985.

Stegassy, Ruth. "John Cupid: We Have Been Called Carnival People: An Interview." *TDR* 42 (1998): 96–107.

Stigler, Elizabeth J. "Trans on the Track: Policing of Gender in the All-Women Space of Flat Track Roller Derby." Presentation, Florida Consortium for Women's and Gender Studies, Boca Raton, April 1–2, 2011.

Stoddard, Tom, and Pops Foster. *The Autobiography of Pops Foster: New Orleans Jazz Man.* Milwaukee: Hal Leonard Corp., 2005.

Stokes, Stephanie. "New Orleans' Iconic Street Tiles Are Falling Victim to Repair Crews." *Times-Picayune,* June 21, 2009. blog.nola.com/news_impact/print .html?entry=/2009/06/olibbp102top2_0622aaa01_y8tile.html (accessed March 15, 2010).

Tallant, Robert. *Mardi Gras . . . as It Was.* 1948. Gretna, La.: Pelican Publishing Co., 1994.

———. "Negroes in the Carnival." *FWP Folder 434* (n.d.).

Tamony, Peter. "Funky." *American Speech* 55 (1980): 210–21.

Taylor, David A. *Soul of a People: The WPA Writers' Project Uncovers Depression America.* New York: John Wiley and Sons, 2009.

Teicholz, Judith. "An Improvisational Attitude: Transforming Painful Patterns through Dyadic Play in Psychoanalysis." Lecture, Tampa Bay Psychoanalytic Society Scientific Meeting, March 6, 2010.

Tucker, Sherrie. "A Feminist Perspective on New Orleans Jazz Women." Research report. New Orleans Jazz National Historical Park, 2004.

———. "Rocking the Cradle of Jazz." *Ms. Magazine* 14 (2004–5): 68–71.

Turner, Kay, and Suzanne Seriff. "'Giving an Altar': The Ideology of Reproduction in a St. Joseph's Day Feast." *Journal of American Folklore* 100 (1987): 446–60.

Turner, Richard Brent. *Jazz Religion, the Second Line, and Black New Orleans.* Bloomington: Indiana University Press, 2009.

VanSpanckeren, Kathryn. "The Mardi Gras Indian Song Cycle: A Heroic Tradition." *MELUS* 16 (1989–90): 41–56.

Vaz, Kim Marie. "Teacher Helps Students Get a Head Start." *Times Picayune,* July 13, 1989. www.canerivercolony.com/CreoleHistory/CreoleHistory.htm#martinez (accessed October 15, 2011).

Ware, Carolyn. "Anything to Act Crazy: Cajun Women and Mardi Gras Disguise." *Journal of American Folklore* 114 (2001): 225–47.

Webb, H. Brook. "The Slang of Jazz." *American Speech* 12 (1937): 179–84.

Wicker, Ragan. "Nineteenth-Century New Orleans and a Carnival of Women." M.A. thesis, University of Florida, 2006.

Wickiser, Ralph L., Caroline Durieux, and John McCrady. *Mardi Gras Day.* New York: Henry Holt, 1948.

Wilkie, Laurie A. "Beads and Breasts: Negotiation of Gender Roles and Power at New Orleans Mardi Gras." In *Beads and Bead Makers: Gender, Material Culture, and Meaning,* ed. Lidia D. Sciama and Joanne B. Eicher. New York: Berg Publishers, 1998. 193–211.

Wilkins, Amy C. "Puerto Rican Wannabes: Sexual Spectacle and the Marking of Race, Class, and Gender Boundaries." *Gender and Society* 18 (2004): 103–21.

Winick, Charles. "How High the Moon: Jazz and Drugs." *Antioch Review* 21 (1961): 53–68.

index